Hidden in Plain Sight

osasere omorodion

Published by osasere omorodion, 2024.

HIDDEN IN PLAIN SIGHT

First edition. December 15, 2024.

ISBN: 979-8218546984

Written by osasere omorodion.

"I walked through hell carrying matches, lit my own fire, and rose from the ashes. I am not here to survive—I am here to ignite."

-Osasere

Table of Content

From the Author
DEDICATION

This book is dedicated to my little feathers—Olivia, Aiva, and Maya. You are why I've soared through the storms of life and the wings that have carried me beyond every limitation. You are the reflection of me. As I write these pages, I know that every word reflects the love, strength, and purpose that you have gifted me. Through the trials, the breaking of generational curses, and the journey of healing, you have kept me grounded and uplifted simultaneously. This story is not just mine—it's for you. For the legacy I leave behind, the truth I uncovered, and the path I've paved so you never have to walk the same roads of uncertainty and pain. I hope that you will always remember the power you carry within and that you, too, will learn to rise, rebel, and embrace the truth hidden in plain sight.

With all my love, Mommy.

INTRODUCTION

Hidden in Plain Sight: The Bare Truth of Authenticity Was Always There is a journey far beyond mere survival. This is my story—Osasere's story—as I am a woman who walked through the fires of life, carrying only the raw power of my truth. Born into a world wrapped in expectation and tradition, I was given a life that seemed decided before I ever opened my eyes. But that path never resonated with me. This memoir is an unearthing, a reckoning, and a call to every reader who dares to look deeper; who knows, there's more than what we've been handed.

This book is not just an account of my struggles; it's a testament to my rise. I peeled back the layers of who I thought I was—layer after layer of conditioning and expectation until I found the core of who I am. This is the story of breaking generational curses, facing down hidden fears, and embracing truths so sharp they could cut. But within that pain lies my power, and this journey has shown me that my strength has always been hidden in plain sight. This book is my rebellion against the silence that tradition imposed upon me, my rejection of every limitation that told me to stay small, to stay quiet, to stay bound.

I am here not to be understood but to ignite, to reveal truths that were never meant to stay buried. My hope is that this story finds you ready, that it awakens within you the courage to reclaim what has always been yours: your authenticity, your power, your freedom. This path of self-awareness and healing is one I walk for myself, for those who came before, and for those who will come after. This is my testament, my legacy—a light to illuminate what's been hidden all along.

CHAPTER 1
Unconditional African

Growing up between two worlds—my Nigerian heritage and the intricate rhythms of American life—was like walking a tightrope. Both cultures shaped me, but they often clashed in ways that left me feeling torn. On one side, Nigerian tradition demanded strict obedience, respect for authority, and an unwavering adherence to family loyalty. On the other, American values of independence and individuality called to me like a distant melody. These conflicting ideals collided with each other in every aspect of my life, creating a tension I carried from an early age. My world was one of duality—tradition and rebellion, love and fear, silence and defiance.

Our home, on the surface, seemed like a haven of cultural warmth and fun. My father's charisma attracted people from all walks of life. He was the kind of man who could light up a room with his presence, commanding attention with ease. To outsiders, he was generous, magnetic, and endlessly charming. But behind closed doors, his duality emerged. At home, he ruled with an iron fist. His anger was sharp and unrelenting, and his discipline left no room for negotiation and self-expression. For my father, control was his way of expressing love, though it was a love I often struggled to recognize. His temper held the silent force of generations—men who had likely carried the same weight of tradition, passing down their pain in the only way they knew how.

My mother, ever loyal, defended him with a devotion that often left me conflicted. "It's our way. This is how it's meant to be," she'd say, her words laced with a mix of resignation and conviction. She justified everything by saying they had it worse, so what we were experiencing wasn't abuse in her eyes. She tried to be the glue that held our family together, using her laughter, cooking, and unwavering prayers to carve out fleeting moments of joy amidst the chaos. But even her warmth couldn't fully shield us from the storm brewing within our walls. Her loyalty to my father, though rooted in cultural duty and love, often blinded her to the harm his actions caused. For her, protecting him meant protecting the family, even when it came at the expense of her children's emotional well-being.

Our house was always bustling with activity. It was known as the hang-out spot. It wasn't just a home; it was a hub, a gathering place for friends, relatives, and even strangers. People came and went as though we lived in an open-door sanctuary, each bringing their own stories and energies. But beneath the surface of this lively façade lay a darker truth. One night, when no adults were home, muffled cries pierced the air. A locked door separated me from what I later came to understand as the rape of a family member. At the time, I didn't fully comprehend what was happening, but the tension in the air was suffocating. My heart raced out of my chest as tears streamed down my face, and I clawed helplessly at the locked door, wishing I could stop what was unfolding. I was helpless to the point of running to my closet to hide and never speaking a word about what I didn't understand was happening. Later, when the truth came to light, it shattered something within me. I felt powerless, haunted by the knowledge that such a horrific act had occurred in the space I called home, a place that was supposed to protect us. That moment marked a turning point, forever altering my view of safety, family, and silence.

That moment awakened an anger in me that I didn't yet know how to name. It was the kind of anger that simmered quietly, growing stronger with time. I realized then that the world wasn't just chaotic—it was cruel. My anger wasn't just about what had happened; it was about the silence that followed, the unspoken rule that we didn't talk about such things. It was the first time I understood the weight of silence as both a shield and a prison. At that moment, I vowed that one day, I would break free.

Living in a home where peace was fleeting taught me to be hyper-vigilant. I learned to read the unspoken cues in a room—the tone of my father's voice, the way his footsteps sounded as he approached, the subtle shifts in energy that signaled when the mood was about to change. This heightened awareness became my survival tool, a skill that would later serve me in life but left me emotionally drained. Suppressing memories became my way of coping. My mind selectively chose what to keep and what to discard, shielding me from the full weight of my trauma. But buried pain doesn't disappear; it festers, waiting for the right moment to resurface.

From an early age, I felt a fire within me—a resistance to the life that was being imposed on me. While others seemed content to accept the status quo, I couldn't. My siblings and I absorbed the chaos of our home in different ways, each of us finding our own way to cope with the turbulence. My younger brother, a gentle Cancer, was my steady companion. He had a calm and nurturing presence that often soothed me when things felt overwhelming. Though quieter than me, he understood the tension in our home and had a way of grounding me with just his presence. In him, I found a quiet ally who reminded me that even amidst the chaos, there was still room for love and connection.

My youngest brother, a Pisces, was different—distant and aloof, retreating into his own world where he could shut out the noise. He wasn't communicative and rarely expressed his emotions, which often left me feeling disconnected from him. Yet, I knew his silence wasn't indifference; it was his way of surviving. He floated through the chaos like a ghost, present but unreachable, and I often wondered what thoughts and feelings lay beneath his detached exterior.

Then there was my older sister, the Aquarius. We didn't get along. As much as I tried to connect with her, our personalities seemed to clash at every turn. She was fiercely independent, stubborn, and unyielding, often refusing my attempts to have a sisterly bond. We argued more than we connected, and at times, it felt like we were speaking entirely different languages. While I wanted to fight against the chaos in our home, she seemed content to create her own rules and stay out of the fray. Her detachment frustrated me, and I often misinterpreted it as indifference. But looking back, I realize it was simply her way of protecting herself.

Each of us carried the scars of our upbringing in our own way. My Cancer brother was my safe space, the one who gave me moments of calm when I needed them most. My Pisces brother, though distant, showed me the power of creating an inner sanctuary when the outside world became unbearable. My sister—though we often clashed—taught me that survival doesn't look the same for everyone and that boundaries are a healthy way of moving forward. Our relationship wasn't easy, but it shaped me, forcing me to confront the reality that love within a family isn't always simple.

At just 13, I discovered an unexpected outlet: braiding hair. It was a skill that came naturally to me, one that required no formal teaching. Braiding became my lifeline, a way to escape the confines of my home while earning my own money. Each braid felt like a small rebellion—a step toward independence and freedom. I found purpose and a sense of control over my life through braiding. It wasn't just about the money; it was about creating something with my hands, something entirely mine, and painting a picture of independence to one day move out. That was when the spirit of motivation was born.

But even as I carved out a path, I knew escaping would require more than physical distance. The cultural obedience demanded in every Nigerian household weighed heavily on me. Authority was enforced through fear, not respect, and questioning it was considered a grave offense. Yet, I couldn't stop asking. Every act of defiance—every time I refused to shrink or conform—felt like a battle against something much more significant than my father's temper. I was fighting against generations of tradition, against the silence and obedience demanded of me.

People called me disrespectful, un-African, rebellious. But I knew that rebellion wasn't just a choice for me but a necessity. It was the only way I could survive. At 21, I finally left home. Walking away wasn't just about physical freedom but about reclaiming my spirit. Leaving meant breaking the chains of fear and obedience woven into my upbringing. It was a declaration that I would no longer be defined by the darkness I was born into.

My parents, despite their flaws, taught me resilience. In them, I saw the strength I admired and the pain I vowed to overcome. Their chains bound them—chains of tradition, trauma, and unhealed wounds. But I refused to let those chains define me. True freedom, I realized, wasn't just about leaving home; it was about healing. It was about confronting the shadows of my past and choosing to break the cycle.

Looking back, I see that my defiance was never just rebellion. Each boundary I set, each act of resistance, was a step toward reclaiming myself. My visible and hidden scars are a testament to my journey. They remind me of the courage it took to face the darkness and choose the light. And though the wounds of my past still linger, they no longer define me. They are a part of my story but not the whole of it. My story is one of transcendence, resilience, transformation, and the unshakable belief that I was meant for something more.

CHAPTER 2
Weight of The World

Some moments don't just change you—they redefine you. They tear away everything you thought you knew and leave you standing at a crossroads, bare and vulnerable. For me, those moments were like a series of storms, each one more intense than the last, demanding that I either break or transform. The universe has a way of testing you, of placing its weight squarely on your shoulders until you have no choice but to look within.

I grew up carrying the pressure of expectations, weighed down by the image of who I was supposed to be. The mold others wanted me to fit was suffocating, and each time I tried to conform, it felt like another piece of myself was slipping away. It wasn't just the world around me that felt heavy—it was the war within me. I didn't know who I was supposed to be, and that lack of clarity left me ashamed, lost, and questioning whether I even had the strength to keep going.

"Shame isn't born from failure—it's born from sacrificing who you are for who the world says you should be."

What I didn't know then was that I wasn't just carrying my own struggles; I was holding a legacy of hidden abilities passed down silently through my family. My grandfather, whose psychic gifts were cloaked in secrecy, had unknowingly passed that lineage to me. As a child, I didn't understand what I was experiencing—the visions, the whispers, the vivid images that seemed to come out of nowhere. Instead of feeling gifted, I felt haunted. The weight of knowing things I couldn't explain made me afraid of my own mind, and that fear became a silent burden I carried everywhere.

The first time I tried to end my life, I was 17. I was in love—or so I thought. My high school boyfriend was my world, my anchor in a life that felt adrift. But what I thought was love was really a bond forged in shared wounds, a connection that mirrored my insecurities rather than healing them. He betrayed me not once, not twice, but twelve times. Twelve betrayals, each one cutting deeper than the last, leaving scars that felt irreparable. I thought if I could just be better—prettier, smarter, more forgiving—he wouldn't hurt me. But with every betrayal, I blamed myself more until I believed I wasn't worth anything at all.

"Love that requires you to lose yourself isn't love; it's a lesson."

That first attempt was the result of heartbreak, yes, but it was also the culmination of years of feeling unseen and unworthy. It was a breaking point I didn't even realize I'd reached. I survived, but the storm within me didn't subside. It lingered, waiting for another moment to pull me under.

Years later, I married a man I thought would bring me emotional stability, a man who seemed consistent and kind. But even on our court wedding day, I felt reservations I couldn't quite name. I ignored them, scared of the ticking clock everyone reminded me of and desperate to create a life I thought I should have. That marriage became another cycle of betrayal, pain, and unmet expectations. I was drowning again, this time with children in the picture, making the weight of it all feel unbearable. The second time I tried to end it, it wasn't heartbreak that drove me—it was the crushing weight of shame, of feeling like I had failed as a wife, a mother, and a person.

And then, there was the third time. I was done asking people for answers, so I turned to the universe. Lying flat on my back, staring up at the endless expanse of the night sky, my heart pounding against the weight of pain and disappointment, I let the tears flow. My right hand stretched across my chest; I felt the rhythm of my heartbeat—a reminder of the life I was desperate to escape yet still tethered to. At that moment, I cried out to God, pleading for a sign—any sign—that my existence mattered, that there was purpose beyond this unbearable ache.

And then it happened. In the vast, infinite universe, in the exact spot where my tear-filled eyes were fixed, a shooting star blazed across the sky. What are the odds? Ask yourself this: have you ever seen a shooting star? How many people can actually say they have? Now imagine the infinite expanse of the heavens aligning at that moment—my eyes locked on the exact place where a star streaked through the darkness as if the cosmos had been waiting just for me. It wasn't just a star; it was a message, a whisper from the universe: "You're not done yet."

From that night forward, I started looking up at the sky every night, searching for reminders that I wasn't alone. Over time, I saw more shooting stars, each one a small light in the darkness, a quiet reassurance that my journey had a purpose. Those stars became my symbols of hope, guiding me back to myself and reminding me that even in my darkest hours, there was still light. That moment under the sky wasn't just an answer—it was the first step in reclaiming my life.

"Sometimes, the smallest light can ignite the fiercest will to live."

Healing didn't come all at once. It was a slow unraveling, a process of facing the pain I had tried to avoid and transforming it into something that could fuel me. My psychic abilities, once a source of fear, became tools for clarity and healing. I began to trust the intuition that had always been there, guiding me even when I didn't understand it. The visions, the whispers—they weren't burdens. They were gifts, showing me that I was connected to something far greater than myself.

For the first time, I felt like I belonged, not to someone else or to the expectations of the world, but to myself. The weight of the world didn't disappear, but I wasn't holding it alone anymore. I had found my strength, not in spite of the pain but because of it.

"Your darkest moments aren't the end—they're the fire that forges your strength. And when you rise, you don't just carry the weight—you carry the light."

CHAPTER 3
The Forbidden Path

I grew up in a world where questioning what we were taught was seen as a threat, a step too close to the edge of what was deemed safe or sacred. Curiosity was considered dangerous, a doorway to things labeled as "witchcraft." Anything outside the lines of tradition was outright forbidden.

But even as a child, I felt a deep hunger for something more—something real, something beyond the boundaries of what I was told to believe. The traditions handed to me felt like walls, not windows. I was drawn to healing modalities that didn't fit neatly into the boxes I'd been given. Crystal healing, energy work, meditation, and numerology made sense to my spirit, even if they didn't align with the world around me. Fear held me back; I was terrified of judgment, afraid of being cast out simply for exploring my truths.

In a world where we're often taught to follow, seeking your answers feels like rebellion. I had to unlearn so much to open my mind and heart to possibilities beyond tradition. For me, this was more than a journey; it was a declaration of freedom. I didn't want to be spoon-fed someone else's version of truth. I needed to taste it, even if it meant facing fear and standing alone. The only way to embrace my spirit was to feed its curiosity, challenging my egoic mind.

Being taught is passive, accepting what others hand you, no questions asked. But seeking? Seeking is courage. It's looking into the unknown with eyes wide open, embracing curiosity over the fear of judgment. It's daring to ask questions.

One of the most pivotal moments in this journey came when I first picked up a book on numerology. To most people in my community, this was blasphemy—a step too far into the realm of the forbidden. But for me, it was like meeting an old friend. The numbers resonated with something deep inside me, whispering truths I hadn't yet fully understood. For the first time, I felt connected to something larger than myself—not through fear, but through knowing.

Through this path, I discovered the power and depth of esoteric wisdom—hidden truths buried beneath layers of dogma and fear waiting to be uncovered. Each door I opened awakened a part I hadn't known existed. I realized there was an entire universe within me, a cosmos that resonated with secrets from ancient wisdom. Astrology, numerology, and alchemy weren't just practices; they were languages that spoke directly to my soul, reminding me of truths I had forgotten but somehow always knew.

In many ways, Esoteric wisdom became the key to understanding the Bible on a new level. It showed me that the Bible is not just a collection of historical stories; it's a book of enlightenment, filled with layers of wisdom, spiritual spells, and ancient teachings hidden in its words. By studying the Hebrew alphabet and its symbolic meanings, I could decode scriptures not as rigid rules but as metaphors and guides for reaching enlightenment. The texts became a map, connecting me to the wisdom within myself and showing me how to bridge intuition and logic—the spiritual with the scientific.

I understood that the Bible was guiding me toward something more profound: that God is not only an external force but also a presence within, a truth in each of us. Through esoteric studies, I learned how spirituality and science come together, leading me to a journey of inner exploration. This wasn't just about following rules or practicing faith out of fear; it was about understanding the divine from within, using logic and intuition to reach God.

One night stands out in my memory—when everything changed. I had been studying the symbolic meanings behind certain scriptures for hours, my mind swirling with revelations. Suddenly, it hit me: everything I had been taught wasn't entirely wrong, but it was incomplete. The stories I had grown up fearing weren't meant to control me—they were meant to empower me. That moment was like stepping into a light I didn't know I needed. The fear began to fade, replaced by a quiet sense of purpose.

Esoteric wisdom doesn't teach you to control the world around you; it allows you to understand it so deeply that it changes your very being. It opens your eyes to the interconnectedness of all things, showing you patterns others miss, revealing that the universe is more magical and complex than we've been led to believe. These truths aren't hidden because they're forbidden but because they're powerful. In seeking them, I found a power within myself that no one could take away.

I had to confront my fears—fears I hadn't even realized were mine, fears passed down in stories meant to keep me safe. Curiosity, I was told, was a sin; asking questions could lead me down a path of darkness. But in those moments, pouring over "forbidden" books and sacred practices, I felt anything but lost. I felt found.

The world tried to tell me that my curiosity was shameful, that my yearning to know and understand was dangerous. But I came to see it as a gift, a spark that lit my way through the shadows of ignorance and fear. I learned that there is no shame in walking a path other people don't understand. The real danger lies in never daring to ask, "What else is there?"

CHAPTER 4
Numbers Don't Lie

I felt an unexplainable pull toward numbers. Not just the everyday counting and measuring—no, this was different. Numbers had a rhythm, a vibration, a language all their own. They carried weight, like echoes from another realm, whispering truths that were hiding in plain sight. At first, I thought it was just a coincidence when certain numbers kept appearing. But over time, I came to understand that numbers are far more than random patterns. They are the universe's way of showing us the blueprint of our lives.

I remember the moment that curiosity truly ignited. I was just entering my healing phase, slowly accepting the idea that I had to be open to everything around me. One day, while working in my salon, I had a conversation with one of my favorite clients. She casually mentioned seeing angel numbers everywhere—222, 111, and so on. I listened, intrigued, as she described how these numbers seemed to follow her. I'd heard of angel numbers before, but I hadn't paid much attention. Yet, something about that conversation planted a seed in my mind. After she left, I started noticing angel numbers, too—almost immediately.

This client became instrumental in my healing process, opening doors I hadn't even known existed. She wasn't just a client; she was a guide sent at the perfect moment. Not only did she teach me about angel numbers, but she also introduced me to my now-favorite artist, Londrelle. His music spoke directly to my soul; each notes soothing wounds I didn't even know were still open. The more I listened, the more I healed. One day, his song "11:11" played at 11:11 am, and I knew it was a confirmation. It felt like the universe was speaking directly to me, saying, *Pay attention. There's something bigger here.*

The numbers became like breadcrumbs scattered through my life, guiding me back to myself. I'd glance at the clock and see 11:11. A receipt would total $22.22. It felt like a cosmic nudge, a quiet reminder that I was being seen and supported. And then, the ringing in my ears began. It wasn't just a sound—it was a signal, a call to be still and pay attention. "We have a message for you," it seemed to say. That was when everything clicked: the universe wasn't just speaking; I was finally listening.

I became obsessed with decoding these messages. Every time I noticed a number, I would pause and ask myself: *What am I feeling? What am I sensing? What am I seeing? What am I thinking? What am I smelling?* This practice helped me stay grounded throughout every signal. It was as if the universe had pressed "pause" on everything around me, inviting me to step fully into the present moment. This practice of stopping, of tuning into every subtle sensory movement, became my way of interpreting the messages beneath the surface of reality. Numbers weren't just signs; they were conversations.

But angel numbers were just the beginning. As I dug deeper, I discovered my Life Path number was a 3. This number embodies creativity, communication, and optimism—qualities I had always felt within me but had never fully claimed. It was a perfect reflection of the depths I craved to express and explore. Suddenly, my life made sense. My constant desire to create, to communicate, to guide others toward understanding wasn't random. It was part of my design, my blueprint. My life wasn't just a series of events; it was a path crafted around self-expression and inner truth.

The deeper I went, the more layers I uncovered. Nameology revealed that my name corresponds to the number 1, the number of leaderships, independence, and originality. It aligned perfectly with my drive to take my own path to lead a life of self-directed purpose. Together, my Life Path 3 and my nameology 1 painted a picture of who I was at my core: a creator, a leader, and a visionary. These numbers weren't just arbitrary; they were reflections of the power I had always carried but hadn't yet fully embraced.

Everything pointed back to the same themes—independence, creativity, and purpose. My name, my birth date, and the numbers that seemed to follow me were like signposts guiding me toward my destiny. They reminded me that I was divinely designed for this journey and that my uniqueness wasn't just a gift—it was the key to fulfilling my purpose.

For me, numbers went beyond being messages. They became tools for release and transformation, helping me let go of what no longer served me and step into the person I was meant to be. They guided me through pain, helping me find purpose in the challenges I faced. Each number carried an energy that moved me forward, urging me to trust the process and the plan that had been laid out for me.

Numbers weren't just random occurrences. They were divine guides, leading me home to myself.

CHAPTER 5
Beyond the Galaxy

As I delved deeper into numerology and unlocked my secrets, I realized there was still more to discover. The numbers revealed patterns and gave me insight into my life's purpose, but something even more significant was calling me—something cosmic. It wasn't just about the numbers anymore; it was about the stars, the planets, and how the universe seemed to hold the blueprint of who I was and who I was meant to be. That's when astrology entered my life, and I began to see the world on an entirely different scale, connecting everything I had learned so far with the essence of who I truly was.

Astrology felt like a natural progression from everything I'd been learning. I had always been fascinated by the idea that the stars and planets could influence our lives, but I hadn't fully understood its depth until I started exploring my birth chart. I began to realize that, just like the numbers, the universe had been communicating with me all along—through planetary movements, through the alignment of the stars at the exact moment I was born. It was like looking at the cosmos and seeing a reflection of myself, of the life I'd led, and even the challenges I had faced growing up.

But stepping into this space wasn't without its struggles. Growing up Nigerian, diving into astrology came with a sense of guilt. In my culture, there is a deep-rooted fear and rejection of anything that steps outside traditional beliefs, especially if it's tied to something like the stars. Astrology was often dismissed as witchcraft, something to be feared and avoided. The moment people hear that I tap into astrology, it feels like a betrayal of the faith and traditions we were raised with. There's this overwhelming sense that I am walking a forbidden path, one that is met with judgment and resistance.

The weight of that guilt was heavy at first, but I knew deep down that I couldn't ignore this calling. My time of birth wasn't just a random detail—it was the key to unlocking my blueprint, the map that revealed who I truly was. My chart didn't tell me what to worship or how to live; it gave me clues about my lessons, challenges, and gifts. It wasn't about abandoning my roots—it was about healing myself and understanding the divine plan that was written in the stars long before I was born.

I remember the first time I studied my birth chart. It was as though I was reading a map of my soul. Every planet, every house, every aspect revealed a different layer of who I was and why I was here. My Sun, sitting in Pisces, explained the sensitivity and depth I had always felt: Pisces, the dreamer, the intuitive, the healer. Growing up in a world where emotions were kept guarded and strength meant to silence, I often felt like an outsider. But this Pisces energy gave me access to something different—a depth and empathy that allowed me to connect with the emotions others wouldn't dare touch. My Sun in Pisces allowed me to feel the energy of those around me, and in a way, it helped me understand my family, even amidst the pain. It gave me an innate ability to heal, not only myself but others, by seeing what lay beneath the surface.

My Moon, in fiery Aries, was the contrast I needed to understand the inner conflicts I often felt. Aries, bold, direct, and passionate, gave me a fire that kept me moving forward, even when life's obstacles felt too heavy. Growing up, this Aries Moon manifested in moments of rebellion, my need to protect, to speak up, to stand against authority that didn't align with my values. It explained the fire that would rise within me in moments of injustice—the need to act, to protect what was sacred to me, even if it went against the softer nature of my Pisces Sun. This combination of water and fire often made me feel conflicted, as though I was simultaneously being pulled in two directions. But astrology showed me that both of these energies were necessary and worked together to create the complexity of who I am—both sensitive and fierce, able to fight for what I believe in while feeling the world around me deeply.

Then there was my Venus, also in Aries, fueling the passion I brought to my relationships. Love for me was never a soft flame—it was an intense fire, all-consuming and transformative. I wanted to dive into the deep end, experience everything, and connect with others in a way that was raw, powerful, and beyond the ordinary. Understanding this placement helped me see why I often loved in ways that others couldn't match and why relationships were always a journey into the depths rather than a casual affair. Growing up in an environment where emotions were hidden, my Venus in Aries gave me the courage to love fiercely, breaking through barriers and embracing a form of connection that was authentic, bold, and unapologetically real.

My Rising sign in Sagittarius is more than just the way I present myself—it's the essence of how the world perceives me and, in many ways, reflects more of who I am than my Sun sign. While the Sun reveals the core of our being and the Moon governs our inner emotional world, the Rising sign is the outer expression of our identity, the energy we exude in every interaction, and the path we walk in life. It's the first impression we leave on others and the foundation of how we approach the world. For me, Sagittarius Rising radiates a sense of adventure, optimism, and endless curiosity. This is the reason I grew up questioning everything. It's the fire that drives me to explore, grow, and embrace life's endless possibilities with an open heart and an expansive mindset. My Sagittarius Rising was the magnetic force that kept pulling me toward expansion, growth, and independence. Sagittarius, the philosopher, and the seeker compelled me to venture beyond what was known and to explore life with boundless possibility. It made me resilient, able to face setbacks and pursue big dreams that others might shy away from. This Sagittarian energy was the reason I couldn't settle; I had to experience life fully and discover truths beyond what I'd been taught. It fueled my need to learn, question, and grow.

Chiron, sitting in my 7th house of relationships in Gemini, was a mirror reflecting the wounds I carried into my connections. Known as the "wounded healer," Chiron represents the areas of life where we feel the deepest pain but also hold the greatest potential for healing and growth. For me, this placement revealed that my greatest lessons would come through relationships—those intimate mirrors that show us not just the beauty but also the shadows we carry within. Relationships, for me, weren't just about love and companionship; they were the crucible in which my soul would transform, teaching me the balance between self-expression and connection.

With Gemini's influence, communication became both my strength and my vulnerability. On the surface, I could express myself well, articulate ideas, and connect with people easily. Yet beneath that surface, there was a lingering struggle to fully communicate my emotional needs and desires. I craved understanding and intimacy, but often felt unheard or misinterpreted. It wasn't just about speaking; it was about finding the courage to voice my innermost truth without fear of rejection or judgment.

Chiron, in this placement, taught me that my wounds weren't just about failed relationships or missed connections—they were rooted in the fear of not being enough, of being misunderstood, or of having my needs dismissed. This fear often led me to hold back to silence parts of myself in an attempt to keep the peace or avoid confrontation. But the more I silenced my truth, the more the wounds deepened, creating cycles of miscommunication and disconnection that left me feeling unseen and unheard.

Healing through Chiron wasn't about finding the perfect partner who could magically understand me; it was about understanding myself. Gemini in the 7th house taught me that communication wasn't just about words—it was about energy, intention, and authenticity. I had to learn to trust my voice, to articulate my needs, and to let go of the fear of being misunderstood. This placement reminded me that true connection starts within and that when I align with my authentic self, the right relationships would naturally follow.

Chiron also revealed that relationships were not meant to be free of conflict or challenge. Instead, they were opportunities to grow, to learn, and to heal. Each connection became a mirror, showing me where I needed to build trust, not just in others but in my ability to express my truth and remain open to the truths of others. It taught me that vulnerability wasn't a weakness—it was the bridge to deeper understanding and connection.

Ultimately, Chiron in Gemini in the 7th House became a guide, showing me that the power of relationships lies not in perfection but in the willingness to grow together. Through this placement, I came to see that my wounds were not a curse—they were an invitation to heal, to grow, and to discover the strength that comes from speaking my truth and embracing my authenticity in every connection.

As I continued exploring, my 9th house in Leo revealed the depth of my need to learn, expand, and express myself boldly. The 9th house represents higher knowledge, spirituality, and exploration, and with Leo sitting here, it infused this area of my life with radiant energy. Leo is the sign of the Sun—bright, powerful, and magnetic. Anything Leo touches expands, bringing light, passion, and vitality. It's where I shine the most, where my presence is undeniable, and where I naturally draw others to me. This placement made my quest for truth and meaning not just a personal journey, but one that inspires others to seek their own answers as well.

In this house of exploration, Leo's influence made it impossible for me to live in the shadows. It gave me the confidence to own my path, to take bold steps toward understanding the world and my place in it. Whether through sharing my experiences, teaching others, or simply embodying my truth, Leo's energy ensured that my spiritual journey would never be small or quiet—it would be expansive, bold, and unapologetically authentic.

This placement also made learning and self-expression deeply fulfilling for me. Knowledge wasn't just something I consumed; it was something I transformed into wisdom, shining a light for others to see. With Leo's influence, I couldn't help but radiate this truth, naturally becoming a guide for those drawn to my energy. It reminded me that the more I embraced my authentic self, the brighter I shined—and the more others were inspired to find their own light.

In my 10th house, ruled by Virgo, I found the reason behind my dedication to building a legacy. Virgo's influence on my house of career and public standing explained my meticulous nature, my hands-on approach, and my commitment to excellence. I wasn't content with shortcuts or superficial success—I needed to build from the ground up, ensuring that every detail was perfect. This placement reflected my journey as a first-generation millionaire, driven to create something meaningful not just for myself, but for those who would come after me.

One of the most affirming parts of my chart is my 2nd house in Capricorn, influenced by Saturn and Neptune. The 2nd house governs wealth, material possessions, and values, and Capricorn's steady, determined energy has always aligned me with financial success. Saturn's influence here emphasizes discipline, structure, and a strong work ethic—traits that have guided me to build wealth methodically and responsibly. At the same time, Neptune's influence in my 2nd house adds a touch of magic, infusing my approach to money with creativity and intuition. This combination of Saturn's grounded energy and Neptune's visionary qualities has allowed me to dream big while staying realistic, attracting wealth in ways that feel both aligned and inspired. My 2nd house taught me that money isn't just a material pursuit; it's an extension of my energy, a reflection of my values, and a tool to create the legacy I'm destined to build.

Then came the powerful influence of my 12th house in Scorpio, with Pluto sitting there like a guardian of hidden realms. The 12th house is the house of the subconscious, the unknown, and the spiritual depths we often avoid. With Scorpio here, it held a profound intensity. Pluto's energy allowed me to face my fears, to understand the cycles of life, death, and rebirth, and to access the healing power of transformation. It connected me to the hidden parts of my psyche, showing me that true strength comes from embracing the depths, not shying away from them.

These placements combined to make me a psychic with a unique array of gifts—clairvoyance (clear seeing), claircognizance (clear knowing), clairaudience (clear hearing), clairsentience (clear feeling), clairtangency (clear touch), and clairempathy (clear emotional feeling). Each house, each sign, and each aspect worked together to open different psychic channels, allowing me to tap into realms beyond the physical and connect with truths hidden from ordinary perception.

Astrology became a language that not only helped me understand myself but also gave me a deeper understanding of life's interconnectedness. It shifted my perspective from asking, "Why is this happening to me?" to, "What am I meant to learn from this?" Astrology didn't make me who I am—it reminded me of who I've always been. My chart wasn't a map to find myself but a reflection of everything already within me. It showed me the patterns and energies at play, the lessons woven into my life, and the strength I carried all along. It wasn't about creating a new identity or relying on something external; it was about aligning with my true essence and trusting the divine design of my path.

The stars didn't give me answers—they held up a mirror. They affirmed the truths I've always felt but couldn't always name, the intuition I'd silenced in the face of doubt or fear. My chart became a reminder that nothing about me is random. The love, the struggles, the questions—all of it was part of something bigger than I could see at the time. Astrology didn't tell me who to be; it reminded me I was already becoming.

What I love most about using astrology to understand and go deeper with my authentic self is that it doesn't trap you in fate or tell you what's coming next. It gives you a deeper understanding of the energy you're working with and how to move through life with intention. It's not about control—it's about freedom. Freedom to embrace every experience as meaningful, every challenge as a lesson, and every triumph as proof of your resilience.

The stars were never dictating my journey; they were guiding me to see the power I already had. And now, I walk with a deeper knowing. My story has always been written in alignment with something greater. The difference is that I finally see it for myself.

CHAPTER 6
Blueprint of the Soul

After my deep dive into numerology and astrology, I thought I had uncovered all I needed to know about myself. But the universe had another layer waiting—a piece to my cosmic blueprint that would bring my life's puzzle into even sharper focus. This discovery was Human Design, a system blending astrology, the I Ching, the Kabbalah, and quantum physics, creating a soul map uniquely tailored to each individual. Human Design doesn't merely outline personality traits; it offers a guide to understanding your core essence, uncovering patterns and aligning with your natural strengths. It's a language, a tool for profound self-understanding, and in this chapter, I want to take you through my own journey with it, sharing how each revelation connected my past, present, and future.

At the heart of my Human Design is my Manifesting Generator type. Manifesting Generators are known as multi-passionate creators, always juggling multiple interests and projects. From the very beginning, this made sense—my life was always filled with numerous ventures, interests, and paths. I could never settle on just one thing, and I used to see that as a flaw, a lack of focus. But learning about my Manifesting Generator energy showed me that this ability to engage with various interests was actually my greatest gift. It explained why I was able to build multiple businesses from the ground up and maintain that momentum. I realized I wasn't meant to walk a single path; I was here to explore and create, to dive into different worlds and connect seemingly unrelated things, and that each endeavor was a crucial part of my journey.

Being a Manifesting Generator also highlighted my natural ability to work efficiently and passionately. This energy type is known for finding shortcuts, making things faster and more efficient. I'd always found myself looking for streamlined ways to achieve goals, whether in business or in personal projects, and learning about this aspect of my design validated why I felt the urge to constantly optimize my life and work. It also explained why I felt resistance to traditional methods; my Manifesting Generator energy pushed me to innovate and improve wherever I went, carving my own way rather than following paths laid out by others.

Another powerful aspect of my design is my Sacral Authority. In Human Design, authority represents how you're meant to make decisions, and Manifesting Generators with Sacral Authority means relying on gut responses and instincts. Throughout my life, I'd often felt conflicted when it came to decision-making, feeling drawn to choices that defied logic but resonated deeply within me. Embracing my Sacral Authority taught me to trust these gut responses without needing rational explanations. My sacral "yes" or "no" became my most trustworthy guide, helping me navigate relationships, career choices, and every twist and turn that life presented. This inner guidance helped me recognize the power of my intuition on a whole new level, teaching me that the answers I seek are always within, waiting for me to listen.

My Defined Throat Center is another crucial part of my Human Design, shaping the way I communicate and express myself. In Human Design, the Throat Center is the manifestation center, where thoughts and intentions come into the world through words and actions. Having a defined Throat Center means my voice naturally has an impact; I am meant to express, teach, and guide others. Throughout my life, I have felt this pull toward speaking out and sharing my experiences and truths. This energy pushes me to communicate in ways that resonate with others, to be a conduit for ideas that uplift and inspire. I've learned to embrace my voice as a gift, realizing that each word I share can shape lives, including my own.

Human Design also introduced me to the concept of Not-Self Themes, particularly frustration and anger for Manifesting Generators. When I'm not aligned with my purpose, frustration and anger become signals, alerting me that I'm off course. Recognizing these themes allowed me to view them differently—not as barriers but as guides, steering me back toward what truly resonates. Over time, I learned that honoring my sacral "yes" and following my passion were the antidotes to frustration and anger. Every time I tried to fit into roles that didn't resonate, I felt drained and uninspired, but aligning with my natural gifts brought a sense of ease and fulfillment.

Deconditioning, a core part of the Human Design journey, became essential for me. Deconditioning involves letting go of societal expectations, familial patterns, and learned behaviors that don't align with our true nature. Embracing my Manifesting Generator energy meant releasing beliefs that I had to follow a linear path, that success meant sticking to one thing, or that my worth was tied to how others perceived me. This process of shedding old beliefs allowed me to embrace the multifaceted nature of who I am and gave me permission to be all of myself unapologetically. It was a journey of self-acceptance, recognizing that every part of me, even the unconventional aspects, was designed with intention.

Each revelation within my Human Design chart became a mirror, showing me the truth of who I am. It allowed me to stop fighting my natural impulses and start honoring them. This system didn't just validate my experiences; it gave me a roadmap to live in alignment with my highest self. With each piece of my design, I saw how my journey, my decisions, and even my struggles were all part of a larger, divinely orchestrated plan. Instead of asking why certain things happened to me, I began to see them as part of my design, each experience a necessary step toward understanding and embodying my purpose.

This shift in perspective—from questioning life's challenges to embracing them as designed experiences—was transformative. Human Design taught me to view my life as a blueprint, carefully crafted and full of meaning. It was no longer about asking, "Why is this happening?" but instead asking, "What am I here to learn from this?" With this newfound awareness, every challenge became a lesson, every joy a gift, and every connection a sacred part of my journey.

CHAPTER 7
Authority Over My Life

Each chapter of my journey brought me closer to a powerful realization: reclaiming authority over my life was not a single moment of clarity but a process—a continuous unfolding. Every discovery, whether through the numbers, the stars, or my own lived experiences, became an essential piece of a larger puzzle. From the traumas I survived in my early years to the profound self-awareness I gained through astrology, Human Design, and introspection, everything pointed toward a single truth: I needed to reclaim myself from the narratives I had inherited, the expectations others had placed upon me, and the limitations I had unconsciously accepted.

For much of my life, I didn't even realize how trauma bonds were holding me back. These bonds—formed through cycles of pain, unmet needs, and emotional dependency—showed up in every corner of my life: friendships, relationships, and even family connections. They disguised themselves as love, loyalty, or responsibility, but at their core, they were built on survival, not growth. It wasn't until I began peeling back the layers of my experiences that I saw the patterns for what they were—unhealthy attachments rooted in shared pain rather than genuine connection.

The truth of trauma bonds is controversial: they often reflect a toxic attachment to a part of ourselves that feels comfortable in chaos. I had to face the fact that I was attached to pain because it was familiar. Breaking away from this meant acknowledging that I had been using these relationships to avoid the real work—the work of facing the parts of me that believed I was only lovable when I was suffering.

In friendships, I often encountered dynamics that reflected deep insecurities—control issues, codependency, and a reliance on external validation. Some of my friends used their beauty as bait, believing it was their greatest or only asset, but it became a barrier to authentic connection. We couldn't relate on a deeper level when it came to manifesting dreams or transforming aspirations into something tangible. There was an unspoken tension, a fear of being left behind, especially as they watched me push forward with a relentless drive to make my goals and aspirations a reality.

Thanks to my Jupiter in Aries in the 5th house, I was naturally equipped with expansive energy when it came to my vision and creativity. The 5th house governs joy, self-expression, and big aspirations, and with Jupiter amplifying this energy in Aries, I had the courage to take risks, the drive to persevere, and the optimism to see my dreams through to completion. This placement wasn't just about dreaming—it was about doing. While others hesitated or doubted, I trusted my instincts and forged ahead. For those around me who struggled with fear or complacency, this energy often created a divide.

Some of these friendships were rooted in their need to keep me close, not because they wanted to see me thrive but because my growth challenged their comfort zone. They needed me to stay "up in them," tangled in their world, where I could serve as their support system, confidant, or even their emotional anchor. My independence and ability to manifest my vision highlighted their own insecurities, and instead of being inspired, they often became jealous or fearful. It wasn't about a lack of love—it was about their own unhealed wounds, which made my growth feel like a threat rather than an opportunity for shared evolution.

Now, I see love and friendship through a radically different lens. I don't seek connections as an escape or a solution to my pain. I've learned that love isn't about filling gaps or silencing inner wounds—it's a conscious choice rooted in freedom, peace, and respect. I no longer need someone to complete me, nor do I crave the intensity that once felt like passion. I have learned to stand fully in my energy, knowing I am whole and enough.

Family trauma bonds were perhaps the hardest to confront. In family dynamics, loyalty is often mistaken for silence, and love is equated with enduring pain. I carried the weight of unspoken expectations and the pressure to maintain harmony at the expense of my truth. I stayed in roles that didn't fit, sacrificing my authenticity to keep the peace. But the peace was an illusion, a fragile facade that crumbled every time I tried to assert myself. Reclaiming authority in these relationships meant challenging the narratives I had been raised with, speaking truths that were uncomfortable, and accepting that not everyone would understand or support my growth. It meant grieving the loss of the family I wished I had while learning to embrace the family I could create for myself.

The common thread in all these trauma bonds was a deep-seated fear of abandonment, a belief that my worth was tied to my ability to endure, to stay, and to give without limits. But as I began to understand these patterns, I realized that true connection doesn't demand self-sacrifice—it invites authenticity. Real love, whether in friendships, relationships, or family, doesn't ask you to betray yourself. It holds space for growth, for honesty, and for the boundaries that protect your energy and peace.

Reclaiming authority over my life wasn't just about breaking these bonds; it was about replacing them with something healthier. It was about learning to set boundaries without guilt, to say no without fear, and to prioritize my own well-being without apology. It meant recognizing that the relationships worth keeping are the ones that honor who you are, not just who you've been.

As I let go of these trauma bonds, I began to attract connections that felt lighter, freer, and more aligned. Friends who celebrated my growth, partners who met me in my truth, and family dynamics that respected my boundaries. These new connections weren't built on survival—they were built on love, respect, and mutual growth. And for the first time, I felt what it meant to be seen, not for what I could give but for who I truly was.

This journey taught me that authority isn't about control—it's about choice. The choice to release what no longer serves you, to embrace what aligns with your truth, and to walk away from anything that dims your light. It's about standing in your power, not because you've never been hurt, but because you've chosen to heal. Reclaiming authority over my life meant reclaiming my relationships, not by forcing others to change, but by changing the way I showed up—for myself, and for the connections I chose to nurture.

This authority wasn't given to me—it was forged in the fires of experience, reflection, and courage. It became a declaration, an unshakable truth: I am no longer confined by the expectations of others. I walk my path with clarity, strength, and purpose, knowing that the design of my life is sacred, and the authority to live it is mine alone.

CHAPTER 8
The Choice That Changed Everything

In every journey, there comes a moment when you are faced with a choice so clear, so defining, that it changes everything. For me, this was not a quiet realization but an undeniable truth that demanded action. I realized that if I didn't protect my peace, honor my path, and set boundaries that reflected my worth, I would remain stuck in cycles that no longer served me. The choice was simple but powerful: I would reclaim my life, piece by piece, starting with myself.

The first step was boundaries—a word that had always sounded distant and harsh but became my saving grace. I began with those closest to me, relationships I once thought were unbreakable. I remember one friend in particular, someone I had shared so much history with but who, over time, began to feel more like a weight than a source of support. Our conversations were one-sided; I was her rock, her sounding board, but she never asked about me. After years of pouring into her without receiving anything in return, I sat in my car one night after an exhausting dinner with her and realized I was pouring from an empty cup. That moment was pivotal—I chose to let go, not out of resentment, but out of love for myself.

This wasn't just about one friendship. I saw a pattern in so many of my relationships. I had been holding onto connections out of loyalty to the past, to a version of myself that no longer existed. It wasn't easy to walk away, but I knew that clinging to these relationships would only keep me tethered to a life I had outgrown. My Aries Venus taught me to love boldly, but it also taught me that real love—whether in friendships, family, or partnerships—must be balanced. Love without reciprocity isn't love; it's self-sacrifice. And I was done sacrificing myself.

The boundaries I set extended beyond relationships and into my career. For years, I had tried to conform to paths that weren't my own, chasing stability in roles that society deemed "secure." I worked 21 different jobs, starting at the age of 13, excelling in each one but feeling disconnected from them all. I tried enrolling in nursing school, becoming a Scrum Master, and even training as a project manager. These paths looked good on paper, but they felt hollow. I remember sitting in a lecture hall during my first week of nursing school, feeling the weight of misalignment. The fast-paced, high-pressure environment was suffocating, and my body rebelled against it. I didn't belong there. No matter how hard I tried to force myself into these molds, life kept pulling me back to my artistry.

Choosing to embrace my creative side wasn't just a career move—it was a reclamation of my identity. Creativity wasn't just something I did; it was who I was. Being an artist meant living boldly, exploring without limits, and expressing myself authentically. I stopped trying to fit into boxes that weren't made for me and started creating my own space. Now, when people ask, "What do you do?" I proudly say, "I'm an artist. Period." And when they press further, I tell them, "I do everything." Because that's what being an artist means—refusing to be confined by anyone else's expectations and honoring the vast potential within me.

As I reclaimed my peace and my path, I noticed how these choices transformed my relationships. I stopped explaining myself to people who didn't understand my journey. I stopped justifying my boundaries to family members who thought I owed them my time and energy. My worth was no longer tied to external validation—it was rooted in the peaceful, authentic life I was building. And while some relationships faded away, those that remained grew stronger, built on mutual respect and understanding.

This choice—the decision to honor myself fully—wasn't easy, but it was the most powerful decision I ever made. It allowed me to step into my power, to create a life that reflected my truth, and to live unapologetically. It wasn't about running away from others or shutting people out; it was about running toward myself. I chose to live in alignment with my purpose, and from that moment on, every step I took was rooted in this truth.

The choice that changed everything wasn't just a decision—it was a declaration. A declaration that my peace, my path, and my purpose were worth protecting. And in making that choice, I reclaimed my life.

CHAPTER 9

From Trauma Bond to True Love

Trauma bonds are insidious. They disguise themselves as love, connection, and passion when, in reality, they are chains forged from shared wounds. These bonds can feel magnetic, unshakable, and even divine. But beneath the surface, they pull us into a cycle of pain that mirrors the unhealed parts of ourselves. Breaking free from these bonds isn't just about leaving a relationship—it's about unraveling the belief systems that keep us attached to them in the first place.

I didn't know I was caught in trauma bonds until I started asking myself harder questions. Why was I drawn to people who left me feeling empty? Why did I mistake chaos for depth and betrayal for love? These weren't easy truths to face, but they were necessary for me to move forward.

One of my most profound realizations was that I had been conditioned to equate love with sacrifice. From a young age, I absorbed the belief that love meant putting others first, even at the expense of my own well-being. This showed up in every type of relationship I had—romantic, platonic, and familial. I thought enduring pain was proof of my devotion, that if I just gave more, I could make the connection work. But the more I gave, the more I lost myself.

Trauma bonds feel intoxicating because they tap into our deepest insecurities. In one relationship, I found myself constantly trying to fix the other person, believing that if I could heal their wounds, they would finally love me the way I craved. But this wasn't love—it was an unconscious attempt to heal my own wounds by pouring my energy into someone who could never reciprocate. The highs and lows of that relationship became addictive, like chasing a feeling that was never meant to last. Walking away wasn't just about letting go of him—it was about letting go of the version of myself that thought I had to suffer to be loved.

Friendships held their own form of trauma bonding. I had friends who thrived on control, jealousy, and codependency. One in particular would often use subtle digs or comparisons to keep me in a space of self-doubt, masking her insecurities with a façade of closeness. When I began manifesting my dreams and achieving milestones she couldn't relate to, the cracks in our friendship became undeniable. What I once saw as a bond of loyalty revealed itself to be an attachment to someone who feared my growth would leave her behind. Releasing these friendships wasn't easy, but it was necessary for my own peace.

Even within my family, I noticed patterns of guilt and obligation that felt suffocating. In my culture, loyalty to family is sacred, and stepping away from those dynamics is often viewed as betrayal. But I realized that love doesn't demand we abandon ourselves. I had to redefine what it meant to love my family while still prioritizing my mental and emotional health. It wasn't about cutting ties—it was about creating new dynamics that respected who I was becoming.

The turning point came when I stopped asking, "Why do they hurt me?" and started asking, "Why do I stay?" That shift forced me to look inward, to confront the parts of myself that were comfortable in chaos. I realized I had been avoiding the void within me, filling it with people who could never truly meet my needs because I wasn't meeting them myself. Breaking trauma bonds wasn't just about saying goodbye to others—it was about saying goodbye to the parts of me that clung to pain as proof of love.

True love didn't come in the form of a partner or a perfect relationship. It came in the quiet moments when I started honoring my own needs, choosing myself over the chaos I had once sought. It came when I learned to say no without guilt, to walk away without fear, and to hold space for my own healing without needing someone else to validate it.

Now, love feels different. It's not a battlefield or a rollercoaster of highs and lows. It's a steady, peaceful presence that uplifts rather than drains. Whether it's the love I share with my daughters, the friendships I now cherish, or the potential for future partnerships, love has become a reflection of the love I've cultivated within myself. It's no longer about filling gaps—it's about sharing wholeness.

One of the most transformative lessons I've learned is that love doesn't have to hurt. It doesn't demand sacrifice or suffering. True love, whether romantic or platonic, respects boundaries, honors individuality, and allows for mutual growth. The relationships I now attract are rooted in authenticity, not obligation. They are built on a foundation of respect, peace, and alignment.

Breaking trauma bonds wasn't the end of my journey—it was the beginning of a new chapter. A chapter where love isn't something I chase but something I create. A chapter where my worth isn't tied to what I endure but to who I am. And in this chapter, love feels expansive, freeing, and deeply aligned with the person I've become.

CHAPTER 10
When the Crown Gets Heavy

Leadership is often glorified—a symbol of triumph, authority, and influence. It's the image of strength many aspire to, but few understand the silent battles it demands. For me, leadership wasn't just about taking charge; it was about owning every piece of my life—the victories, the failures, the growth, and the mess. Wearing the crown of self-leadership was the most profound journey I'd embarked on, but no one prepared me for how heavy it would feel.

From a young age, I was thrust into the role of mediator, fixer, and guide. In family dynamics, friendships, and even my early jobs, people saw me as someone who could carry the weight for everyone else. But what happens when the person who holds everyone else up is left standing alone? I poured my energy into others, and while they thrived, I felt myself slipping away. The crown I wore wasn't chosen—it was placed on me by circumstances and expectations I didn't fully understand. I didn't just need to lead others; I needed to learn how to lead myself.

My entrepreneurial journey began as a way to claim independence, but it quickly became a labyrinth of lessons and challenges I wasn't prepared for. What started as a small hustle with herbal products and sea moss evolved into a global enterprise during a time when the world seemed to be shutting down. I became the first in my family to hit millionaire status, scaling a business that others could only dream of. Orders poured in, employees relied on me, and my Manifesting Generator energy turned opportunities into results with remarkable speed. It felt like I was unstoppable.

But with every milestone, the pressure mounted. I wasn't just running a business—I was trying to be everything for everyone. A wife, a mother, a leader, a mentor. I'd built a life of abundance, but it came with sacrifices I didn't anticipate. The weight of responsibility grew heavier with each passing day. The business thrived, but my spirit wavered. The monthly revenue soared to $60,000, but the cracks in my foundation were impossible to ignore. The success that had once felt liberating began to feel suffocating.

When my marriage fell apart, it was like the ground beneath me shattered. The crown I'd been wearing felt unbearable. I found myself at a crossroads, questioning everything I'd built. Isolation became my only refuge. I stepped away from friends, family, and even social media, retreating into the quiet to find clarity. In the silence, I realized that I had spent years building a life for others, but now it was time to build one for myself.

Choosing to lead myself wasn't just a decision—it was a reckoning. I had to confront the stories I had told myself about what success looked like, what strength meant, and what I truly valued. Leadership wasn't about how much I could endure for others—it was about finding the courage to say no, to let go, and to prioritize my peace. The crown wasn't something I could give up, but I could learn how to carry it differently.

I began by redefining my boundaries. I let go of relationships that drained me, no matter how long they had been a part of my life. I stepped back from roles and commitments that didn't align with my purpose. These weren't easy choices; they were sacrifices that came with grief and uncertainty. But each boundary I set was a declaration of self-respect, a step toward reclaiming the parts of myself I had lost.

In this process, I discovered that leadership isn't about control—it's about alignment. I stopped trying to meet the expectations of others and started listening to the quiet voice within me. My Human Design, with its Sacral Authority, became a guide. Every gut instinct, every intuitive nudge became a compass pointing me toward the life I was meant to live. For the first time, I trusted myself fully, even when the path ahead seemed unclear.

The weight of the crown taught me invaluable lessons. I learned that leadership doesn't mean having all the answers—it means being willing to ask the right questions. It means standing firm in your truth, even when others don't understand. It means choosing peace over perfection, authenticity over approval, and growth over comfort. Leading myself meant embracing the parts of me that were still healing, still learning, still growing.

As I stepped into this new understanding of leadership, my relationships shifted. Some faded away, unable to meet the new standards I had set for myself. Others deepened, built on mutual respect and shared values. I no longer needed to prove my worth through what I could give or endure. My energy became sacred, and I chose to share it only with those who honored it.

The journey wasn't easy, but it was necessary. I came to understand that the crown's weight wasn't a burden—it was a responsibility. A responsibility to myself, to live fully and authentically, no matter how heavy it felt at times. And as I carried it, I found a freedom I had never known. Freedom to be unapologetically myself, to create a life that felt true, and to lead not just with strength but with grace.

This chapter of my life wasn't about achieving more or doing more—it was about being more. Being more aligned, more present, more at peace. The crown still rests on my head, but now it feels like a symbol of the life I've claimed for myself, a life guided not by others' expectations but by my truth. And in carrying it, I've found the courage to lead myself, not as a reflection of what the world wants, but as the fullest expression of who I truly am.

CHAPTER 11
Echoes of Death

The weight of leadership had pushed me to my limits, but there was another kind of weight I had carried far longer—the unspoken grief of my body, my choices, and my losses. Even as I stood firm in my boundaries and decisions, there were moments that revisited me like ghosts, reminders of a pain I hadn't fully processed. The crown I wore in life was heavy, but so too was the burden of past choices and silent suffering. Leadership was one thing—this was another.

It all came rushing back as I was haunted by the memories of me sitting in that cold, sterile room. Nervous energy raced through my veins, my pulse pounding in my fingertips. The sterile air, the bright lights, the faint hum of machines—it was all too familiar. *How did I end up here again?* I thought, the question heavy with regret. This wasn't my first time here. The weight of knowing what was about to happen pressed down on me, suffocating and unrelenting.

"Please don't think. Don't think." The mantra spun in my head as I tried to silence the chaos within me. I forced my breath to steady, but my hands trembled in my lap. "Osasere, you're up first!" the nurse called, her tone clinical yet kind. Her words snapped me out of my haze, but my feet felt like lead as I stood. Clothed only in a hospital gown and those cold, grip-bottomed socks, I shuffled toward the bed. Each step felt like a reckoning, my heart sinking deeper into my chest.

I climbed onto the bed, the chill of the metal against my skin making me shiver. "Please lay down, and we'll strap your hands," the nurse instructed softly. "The procedure will take about 10 minutes. The doctor will be in shortly." Her words were meant to comfort me, but they only heightened my anxiety. Lying there, restrained, I felt like a sacrificial offering—vulnerable, exposed, and fighting back the tears that threatened to spill. One escaped, tracing a path down my cheek, and I turned my head, wishing the ground would swallow me whole.

The doctor walked in, his demeanor calm and composed. "You're in good hands," he said, his attempt at reassurance falling flat. As they injected the sedative, the nurse leaned over and whispered, "It's time to sleep." I focused on a butterfly mural on the ceiling, its vibrant colors a stark contrast to the sterile room. The clock read 8:06... 8:06... 8:06. The numbers repeated in my mind, a strange rhythm until everything faded to black.

I woke up in searing pain, though numbness followed soon after. It wasn't the first time getting an abortion, but the weight of it all was as crushing as ever. Next to me, a young girl sobbed, looking as though she were barely out of childhood. Her pain reignited my own memories. I remembered my first time: broken, numb, barely alive—a ghost of myself. I had carried life six times, each time a different story, a different hope. Three blessings, two abortions, and one miscarriage. Each loss had left a scar, a wound that felt impossible to heal.

One memory, in particular, tore through me like a storm: the miscarriage. For 96 hours, I cried without stopping, unable to eat, unable to sleep. The betrayal was fresh; I had just learned my partner was living a double life, tangled in lies and infidelity to levels beyond my understanding. His double life of sleeping with prostitutes, strippers, and gambling addictions. I lay there for days, blood spotting my bed, pain relentless. Then I mustered the strength to go to the emergency room.

"I'm sorry, there is no baby," the doctor had said. It was a declaration that shattered what little resolve I had left. Whether through miscarriage or termination, death had found its way to me yet again.

In those moments, it felt like death owned me. The death of the spirit, the death of hope, the death of love—it feels like hell's fire branding itself into you. But I've learned that it doesn't own you forever. We are human, and every experience in life has the potential to make us wiser, stronger, and more whole. My rebirth began when I chose to forgive myself and to stop carrying the weight of those lost dreams as my only story.

One day, I found myself alone in a park, staring at the sky with tears streaming down my face. I pleaded for mercy, for forgiveness, for release from the agony I had carried like a second skin. It was there, beneath the open sky, that I began to write letters to each life I had carried. Each word poured out of me like a flood, an apology, a prayer, a hope for redemption. I asked for forgiveness from each soul that had once been a part of me. My tears blurred the ink, but I kept writing until the weight began to lift.

In that moment, I realized that forgiveness wasn't just about those lives I had lost—it was about forgiving myself. It was about releasing the shame and guilt that had shackled me for so long. If I wanted to be a whole mother to my three daughters—my feathers, my future queens—I had to let go of the regret that had kept me bound. How could I teach them to see themselves as royalty, to stand tall and strong, if I still carried regret like a ball and chain?

Forgiveness opened the doorway to peace, and it was peace that I chose for myself. I decided not just to go through the pain but to grow through it. Every scar, every heartbreak, became the foundation of my strength. I began to see the mercy and opportunity that life had given me, and if God could grant me that grace, who was I to withhold it from myself?

The crown I wore as a leader in my own life had never felt heavier, but this time, it didn't break me. Instead, it reshaped me. I found the courage to breathe deeply again, to smile genuinely, to let go of the weight that had once felt like my entire world. I chose to live—not just survive but truly live. I embraced myself, whole and unbroken, and in doing so, I found the freedom to love my daughters and myself fully.

This was my rebirth, my rise from the ashes. And in that moment, I knew I was unbreakable.

CHAPTER 12
My Bosses Call Me Mommy

Motherhood didn't just change my life; it redefined it. My journey to becoming a mother was layered with complexity—trauma, growth, and rebirth. Yet, through the challenges, I found a love so profound that it altered my entire being. My three daughters, my little feathers, bring color, wisdom, and light to my life, teaching me lessons I never imagined. They are not just my children; they are my greatest teachers, mirrors reflecting the depths of my spirit and my strength.

As a single mother, I've worn every hat imaginable—provider, protector, guide, and most humbling of all, student. Each role has forced me to dig deeper into myself, confronting vulnerabilities while discovering reservoirs of resilience I didn't know existed. Raising daughters comes with a unique spiritual weight as if the universe placed them in my life to teach me what I needed to heal, reclaim, and embrace. They each carry a piece of my essence, reminding me of who I am and challenging me to grow in ways I never anticipated.

Motherhood has brought the influence of my Jupiter in Aries in the 5th house into sharp focus. This placement emphasizes courage, expansion, and creativity in all things related to children and personal expression. Jupiter's energy has guided me to understand the dynamic assignment of raising my daughters—not just as their mother but as their spiritual guide. Aries' boldness fuels the way I nurture their individuality, encouraging them to embrace their identities without hesitation. With

Jupiter's expansive energy, I see motherhood as a playground of limitless possibilities, where my children can grow into their fullest selves. This placement also grants me the optimism and drive to navigate the challenges of parenting with unwavering faith in our collective journey.

Each of my daughters reflects a unique aspect of my soul, creating a dynamic and vibrant family unit that feels both sacred and transformative. My eldest, A Gemini Sun and Pisces Rising, embodies my spiritual psyche with her deep empathy and emotional intelligence. She connects with the world on a soul level, reminding me of the power of vulnerability and the importance of keeping my heart open. She often mirrors the part of me that sees beyond the surface, helping me remain grounded in compassion.

My middle daughter, Scorpio Sun and Scorpio Rising, is the bold firecracker of the family—fierce, fearless, and determined. Her energy feels like a reflection of my inner drive, the part of me that relentlessly pursues my dreams and refuses to back down. She is structured, tenacious, and unapologetically herself, reminding me that life is meant to be lived boldly and with purpose.

My youngest daughter, Sagittarius/Capricorn Cusp Sun and Gemini Rising, carries an innate love for beauty, humor, and self-expression. She has a brilliant mind and a natural eye for aesthetics and brings lightness to our home through her infectious laughter and joy. In her, I see the part of me that cherishes life's pleasures, intellects, and luxuries—the part that reminds me to pause, appreciate, and celebrate the small, beautiful moments.

In our home, we've built our own traditions—ones that honor individuality, creativity, and self-expression. Growing up, rigid rules and expectations bound me, but I've chosen to raise my daughters in a space where freedom and authenticity thrive. One of the ways this manifest is through our embrace of nudity as a form of self-acceptance. Nudity in our home isn't about exposure; it's about freedom, trust, and honoring our bodies as sacred vessels. I want my daughters to see their bodies as beautiful and powerful, free from the shame and judgment the world often imposes.

By normalizing nudity, I'm teaching them that their bodies are not objects to be hidden, misused, or critiqued but sacred expressions of who they are. This practice has created a sense of openness in our home—a space where we don't have to hide, emotionally or physically, to feel loved and accepted. It's a tradition I wish I'd been given as a child, and I'm proud to pass it on to them.

Self-expression is at the heart of our family dynamic. I encourage my daughters to explore who they are without fear of judgment. Whether it's through the way they dress, the hobbies they pursue, or the beliefs they hold, I want them to know that their individuality is celebrated. In this house, there is no such thing as "too much"—there is only what feels authentic to you. By fostering this freedom, I'm raising daughters who are not only confident but also deeply connected to their own truths.

Of course, the world has its opinions. People have tried to box me in, whispering what a "good mother" should look like. "You're a mom; you shouldn't dress like that." "Focus on practicality, not your passions." But I've learned to silence those voices. My sensuality, ambition, and self-expression don't detract from my motherhood—they enrich it. I'm showing my daughters that they can be anything they want to be and live boldly without apology.

I've faced criticism, but I've come to understand that true leadership is often controversial. Real change-makers challenge the status quo, and that's exactly what I aim to do—not just for myself but for my daughters. I want them to see that confidence isn't about conforming to expectations; it's about standing firm in your truth and living authentically, no matter who approves.

Analyzing my astrology chart and how it showed up in parenthood was an enlightening experience. Jupiter represents expansion, abundance, and wisdom, guiding us to embrace opportunities for growth and to live with optimism and purpose. The 5th house represents creativity, self-expression, joy, romance, and the nurturing of what we create, including children, passion projects, and our unique talents. It's where we explore the pleasures of life and connect with the essence of our individuality.

Jupiter's influence in my 5th house gives me the wisdom to see motherhood as more than just nurturing—it's about empowering my children to stand tall in their own light. It's the courage to guide them without smothering them, to teach them to trust their own intuition, and to let them explore the world with a sense of wonder and adventure. This placement reminds me that my role isn't to dictate their path but to create an environment where they can discover it for themselves.

Every day, I demonstrate to my daughters that strength isn't just about enduring challenges—it's about thriving despite them. Together, we are breaking cycles, building legacies, and creating a life that honors who we are, not what the world expects us to be. My daughters aren't just watching—they're learning, growing, and becoming the queens they were born to be.

Motherhood has been my greatest challenge and my greatest gift. It has taught me to lead with love, to think independently, to trust my instincts, and to embrace the fullness of who I am. My daughters are my legacy, my feathers, and my greatest inspiration. Through them, I've learned that true leadership isn't about control—it's about creating a space where others can rise. And as I watch my daughters grow into their own power, I know that the crown I wear as their mother isn't just heavy—it's worth every ounce of its weight.

CHAPTER 13
I'll Blow Your Mind

I was born on February 20, sharing a cosmic alignment with Rihanna—a Pisces Sun with an Aries Moon. Our shared astrological energy resonates deeply: water's intuition paired with fire's boldness. This dynamic embodies creativity, sensuality, and unapologetic self-expression. Like Rihanna, I am a woman born to defy convention, but my journey to embracing this truth was far from straightforward.

In my world, sensuality wasn't celebrated; it was silenced. I was taught to hide my sexuality, to see it as something shameful, something to be controlled and contained. Society's gaze weighed heavily on me, constantly dictating what a "good woman" should be: modest, reserved, almost invisible. The message was clear—my body was a liability, my desires were dangerous, and my expression of self was something to be subdued.

But deep down, I've always seen sex as more than an act. To me, it is art—a sacred dance of energy, intention, and creation. Sex is not just physical; it's emotional, spiritual, and deeply transformative. It's a language that communicates without words, a force that connects souls and mirrors truths we often hide from ourselves. It's the purest form of vulnerability and power, an interplay of surrender and dominance, softness and strength.

For years, I carried this understanding quietly, afraid of how it would be received. The weight of societal expectations made me question myself, forcing me to deny parts of who I was. I downplayed my sensuality, dimmed my light, and buried my desires under layers of shame. But no matter how much I tried to suppress it, the truth remained: sensuality is an essential part of my being, as intrinsic to me as the air I breathe.

The journey to reclaiming this part of myself began with unlearning everything I had been taught about sex and sensuality. I realized that the shame I carried wasn't mine—it was a product of cultural conditioning, a tool used to control women and disconnect them from their power. I had to rewrite the narrative, to see my sensuality not as a weakness but as a source of strength and creativity.

When I began to embrace this truth, everything changed. I started to see my body as a masterpiece, a vessel through which I could express my spirit and connect with the divine. Every curve, every sensation, every movement became a celebration of life itself. I stopped hiding and started honoring the connection between my sensuality and my spirituality. This wasn't about pleasing anyone else—it was about reclaiming the parts of myself that had been silenced for too long.

Sex, for me, is an art form, a practice of presence and intention. It's about more than physical pleasure; it's about energy exchange, about creating something sacred with another person. When approached with love, trust, and intention, sex becomes a powerful tool for healing and transformation. It's a way to release pain, to connect deeply, and to experience the divine within ourselves and each other.

In embracing my sexuality, I also discovered the importance of boundaries. My sensual energy is sacred, and not everyone deserves access to it. I learned to be discerning, to honor my body and my spirit by sharing them only with those who respect and value me fully. This shift wasn't just about protecting myself—it was about stepping into my power, about owning my desires without shame or apology.

Now, I walk through life with a different energy. I am unapologetically sensual, fully aware of the power that lies within me. I no longer shrink to make others comfortable, nor do I hide the parts of myself that society deems too much. My sensuality is mine to own, explore, and express in whatever way feels authentic to me. My worth is not determined by anyone's comfort with my presence; I am a force in my own right, unafraid to stand fully in my own power. I am the embodiment of fire and water, sensuality and spirit, strength and vulnerability. I am here to be seen, to make a statement, and to challenge every limit that has been set for me.

This chapter of my life is about freedom—the freedom to be fully myself, to honor my desires, and to live without compromise. I am the perfect balance of fire and water, strength and vulnerability, sensuality and spirituality. And if that challenges the world's expectations, then so be it. I am not here to fit in; I am here to blow your mind.

When I enter a room, I no longer shrink to make others comfortable. I carry the weight of my presence, allowing my energy to flow freely and unapologetically. My worth is not determined by anyone's comfort with my presence; I am a force in my own right, unafraid to stand fully in my own power. I am the embodiment of fire and water, sensuality and spirit, strength and vulnerability. I am here to be seen, to make a statement, and to challenge every limit that has been set for me.

If that makes others uncomfortable, then so be it. I am not here to fit into anyone's expectations; I am here to blow your mind.

CHAPTER 14
Journey Through the Walls

Sensuality, for me, became a tool for reclaiming the parts of myself I once suppressed—a power I chose to embrace unapologetically. But as I explored this energy more deeply, I began to realize it wasn't just about expression; it was about intention. My sensuality wasn't meant to be scattered, given freely to those who couldn't honor it. It was sacred, a divine force that deserved preservation and purpose. And so, my journey evolved. What started as an external celebration of my essence shifted inward toward a reclamation of my energy, my spirit, and my body. The next step in my journey wasn't about diminishing this power—it was about protecting it, honoring it, and redefining what it meant to share it.

Journey Through the Walls—not barriers built of stone or glass, but something far deeper, something sacred. These are the walls of my being, my body, my temple, and ultimately, my choice. This is the story of reclaiming the core of who I am, honoring the sanctity of my flesh and spirit through the profound act of celibacy. This isn't about avoidance or fear. It's about reclaiming my essence, preserving the magnetizing, transformative energy within me, and choosing to share it only with a soul who truly values it—a deserving king who understands the worth of my temple.

For too long, I didn't understand the weight of letting undeserving men into my sacred space. I lost my virginity at just 13, an age when

I was still discovering myself but was pressured by a world that tied a woman's worth to her sexuality. My first long-term relationship deepened this narrative. He "turned me out," teaching me to equate my value with my ability to perform and satisfy. Sex became an art form, yes, but it was an art I misused—a canvas painted with desperation for validation and worth.

Every partner left an imprint, an invisible energy that lingered long after they were gone. I began to notice the effects—not just emotionally but physically and spiritually. Projects that once flowed effortlessly began to stall, businesses struggled, and my energy felt fractured. My light, once so brilliant and expansive, dimmed under the weight of these entanglements. I realized that with each connection, I was absorbing not only their energy but also their fears, limitations, and unresolved pain. I was giving away pieces of myself, allowing my sacred energy to be drained by those who didn't see its value.

Choosing celibacy was not a retreat but a radical act of self-love and empowerment. This decision wasn't about abstaining from sex—it was about reclaiming my peace, clarity, and self-worth. In a society that often equates a woman's value with her sexual availability, celibacy is seen as an anomaly, even a rebellion. But for me, it became a declaration of my sovereignty. It allowed me to set a standard for who and what I would allow into my life, filtering out those who couldn't meet me at my level of intentionality and depth.

The world will tell you that celibacy might push people away, that it's isolating or impractical. I've heard the whispers and felt the judgment. But to me, celibacy became a powerful shield, revealing the truth about those who approached me. If a man couldn't honor my decision to preserve my energy and sacredness, then he was never meant to walk this path with me. My temple is not for everyone—it is reserved for a union rooted in mutual respect, growth, and legacy.

This choice redefined how I viewed myself and my worth. My body, my energy, and my spirit are not commodities to be given freely—they are treasures to be cherished. In choosing celibacy, I wasn't closing myself off; I was opening myself to a deeper connection with my purpose and my higher self. This wasn't about depriving myself but about enriching my life, channeling my energy into creative pursuits, personal growth, and the dreams I am building for myself and my daughters.

Celibacy also helped me heal the wounds I didn't know I was carrying. It gave me the space to confront the traumas and patterns that had led me to seek validation through physical connections. With every day of this journey, I have dismantled the narratives that once ruled me—that my worth was tied to how much I could give and that my value was determined by my ability to please.

As I reclaimed my energy, I felt my manifesting powers return. My mind became clearer, my intentions sharper, and my light brighter. I channeled my energy into my businesses, my artistry, and my legacy. I stopped seeking external validation and began to find fulfillment within myself. My choice to honor my sacred space became a catalyst for growth and transformation, allowing me to step into the fullness of who I am.

In this journey, I've created a sanctuary within myself—a place of peace, power, and purpose. My body is not just mine but a vessel of creativity, healing, and divine energy. I hold it as sacred, knowing that the man I chose to share it with met me not just on a physical level but on a spiritual and emotional plane. He valued his own energy as much as I value mine, and together, we built something extraordinary—a union that expands, uplifts, and honors the legacy we are meant to create.

Celibacy has taught me that my body, my energy, and my spirit are sacred gifts, not to be given away but to be shared intentionally and purposefully. It has allowed me to embody the woman I have always known I could be—strong, unapologetic, and deeply in tune with my purpose. This journey is not about denying myself but about choosing myself every day, knowing that this choice aligns me with the love, respect, and legacy I deserve.

This is my journey through the walls—walls that protect my sacredness, walls that honor my worth, and walls that invite only those who see the beauty and power within. When the time came to let someone into this sacred space, it wasn't an act of compromise but an expansion of everything I have built within myself. It was a union that reflects the love, light, and legacy I have cultivated, a testament to the power of honoring oneself fully.

CHAPTER 15
Love vs Limerence

Love and limerence. At first glance, they may seem indistinguishable—a whirlwind of emotions, intensity, and connection. But their essence could not be more different. Love is a steady flame; it grows roots, nourishes the soul, and stands as a partnership built on mutual respect and trust. Limerence, on the other hand, is a wildfire—burning bright, consuming everything in its path, only to leave behind emptiness. It is obsession masked as connection; a hunger fueled by fantasy rather than reality.

"Love is a choice rooted in mutual growth; limerence is a craving born from emotional highs."

The illusion of limerence is seductive. It sweeps you up and makes you believe it's everything you ever wanted, only to drain you dry. I mistook this illusion for love more times than I care to admit. Limerence is intoxicating—an obsession that disguises itself as connection, an addictive game where you convince yourself that if you give enough, they'll stay. But here's the truth: limerence isn't love. It's an insatiable hunger, a hollow need that promises validation but leaves you starving for more.

I had to learn this distinction the hard way. For years, I mistook the intoxicating pull of limerence for love, confusing the fiery thrill of being wanted with the quiet, steady warmth of being cherished. Limerence had its hooks in me, exploiting my need to feel seen, wanted, and consumed. I chased its promises of validation, diving headfirst into relationships that only left me emptier. It wasn't love; it was a mirage, a mirror reflecting the wounds I hadn't yet healed within myself.

"Limerence is not about connection; it's about attachment to a fantasy."

Limerence is an illusion that thrives on our deepest insecurities. It is the flutter in your chest when they text back, the desperation to decode every word and gesture as proof of your worth. It's the thrill of anticipation, the high of being chosen—but it's fleeting, conditional, and dependent on how well you can perform to keep the connection alive. I lived in this cycle for too long, giving parts of myself away to chase the fleeting intensity of limerence, believing that if I just loved harder, gave more, or proved myself, I could turn it into something real.

"True love invites you to grow; limerence demands that you chase."

Breaking free from limerence required me to confront myself. It wasn't about the other person; it was about me. I had to face the parts of myself that believed love had to be earned, that equated intensity with passion, and that sought validation in someone else's eyes. I had to dismantle the idea that love was about being needed rather than being valued.

True love, I've come to realize, feels like coming home to yourself. It's a safe space where you can stand in your fullness, imperfections and all, without fear of rejection. Love is freedom, not bondage; it's mutual respect, not dependency. It doesn't ask you to lose yourself but encourages you to become even more of who you truly are.

"Limerence thrives on insecurity; love grows from a foundation of self-worth."

When I began to love myself, I gained the discernment to recognize real love when it arrived. True love doesn't need to be chased; it meets you where you are, and together, you rise. It is rooted in reciprocity, grounded in reality, and nurtured by shared purpose. It is a partnership that honors boundaries celebrates individuality and thrives on mutual respect.

"Limerence is fleeting; love is enduring."

Walking away from limerence was an act of rebellion, a decision to reclaim my life. I stopped searching for someone to complete me and started becoming whole on my own. I realized that my worth isn't tied to my ability to be needed, desired, or adored. My worth is inherent; it's something that no one else can give or take away. I am enough as I am, without the highs and lows, without the endless search for validation.

In embracing true love—love for myself—I let go of the need to prove, to chase, to be consumed by anyone but my own growth. Self-love is not selfish; it is the foundation upon which all other love is built. I no longer need someone else to fill the gaps; I am whole. And from this place of wholeness, I know that any love I welcome into my life will be a choice, not a necessity—a reflection of my completeness, not an attempt to fill a void.

So here I stand, no longer addicted to the emotional highs of limerence, no longer sacrificing myself to feel loved. I am choosing love that is steady, that is real, and that allows me to be fully myself without compromise. This is the love I deserve—the love that holds space for growth, that honors boundaries, and that recognizes my worth without asking me to prove it. It's a love that reflects my own self-acceptance, and that sees me as a whole, just as I am.

"In the end, love doesn't complete us—it complements the strength we've built within ourselves."

And that, I've found, is the most powerful love of all.

CHAPTER 16
Heal in Private Glow in Public

The journey from limerence to love wasn't just about reshaping how I saw relationships—it was also about reclaiming how I saw myself. After years of seeking validation from others, I realized the most profound relationship I'd ever have was the one with myself. Love—real love—demanded that I turn inward to heal the parts of me that limerence had fractured, not for an audience but for myself.

As I began this inner work, it became clear: healing is not meant to be a spectacle. The most transformative moments of growth happen in silence, away from the noise of the world and the need to prove or explain. Healing privately gave me space to re-center and release, to redefine my identity not as someone broken by her past but as someone reshaped by it.

In a world obsessed with exposure and validation, I chose something radical: to heal in private. This isn't about secrecy; it's about sacredness. It's about holding my journey close and understanding that not every scar needs a stage and not every wound requires an audience. Healing in silence became my way of preserving the purity of my transformation—guarding it against judgment, misunderstanding, and the unsolicited opinions that often cloud the vulnerable process of becoming whole.

"Not every battle is meant for display; some wars are won in the quiet trenches of the soul."

I learned this truth early, in moments when the world demanded explanations, even as I was still finding my footing. Healing in private isn't hiding; it's protection. There are wounds too sacred to expose and truths too heavy for those unprepared to carry their weight. This act of keeping my healing sacred taught me discernment—who I allowed into my inner world and who I didn't.

We live in a society that glamorizes struggle as though pain must be paraded for it to be valid. The struggle becomes a spectacle, resilience a commodity, and personal triumph is often reduced to a hashtag. Strength, in its raw and honest form, isn't about being seen. It's built-in solitude, in the unseen moments when no one is there to applaud your victories. True strength doesn't require witnesses; it is born in silence, where you gather the fragments of yourself and rebuild.

My glow—the quiet confidence, the radiant presence—is the result of these invisible wars. I didn't arrive at this light because I sought validation from others. I arrived because I chose to sit with my pain, to understand it, and to turn it into a source of power. For too long, we've been told that sharing our struggles is essential to connection as if our worth hinges on how much we reveal.

But here's what I've learned: my healing, my scars, my pain—they belong to me. They are not stories for others' consumption or tools for their comfort. Healing in private became my rebellion against a culture that craves every detail, even the most vulnerable, and turns it into a spectacle.

"When you protect your journey, you preserve your strength."

This became my mantra. I don't owe anyone the story of my scars, the battles I fought alone, or the sleepless nights spent trying to rebuild myself. The world sees my glow, but they will never know the storms I endured to carry this light. And that's exactly how it should be. My radiance is not a product for public consumption but a testament to re-silience cultivated away from the noise.

Each scar, each untold story, is a private chapter in a book only I hold. I healed in silence so I could stand in power, not defined by my pain but transformed by it. When I walk into a room, I carry not just my presence but the quiet victories, the sacred battles that shaped me. My glow isn't accidental; it's earned. It's the light of a woman who chose to do the hard work, not for an audience, but for herself.

"Some things are meant to remain unshared. The world may see the light that radiates from me, but they will never understand the journey it took to shine."

Healing in private gave me back my narrative. It allowed me to rise, not as someone defined by her struggles but as someone who chose to honor her journey on her terms. My glow is my proof—a steady, silent reminder that not every battle needs an audience and that the most profound transformations happen in the spaces where no one is watching.

Let people speculate. Let them wonder. I've learned to protect the sacredness of my journey, to guard the spaces that allowed me to heal. My glow is irreplaceable because it's mine. It's a strength forged in silence and carried with pride, a strength that doesn't require anyone else's understanding.

I chose to heal in private so that I could glow in public—a glow that is my legacy, a testament to the resilience and grace of a woman who dared to rebuild herself in peace. Let the world see the light, but let them never forget that light was born in the quiet, cultivated with love, and carried forward with unshakable resolve.

CHAPTER 17
Eternal Rest

The journey to peace wasn't a destination I stumbled upon; it was a battle I fought, layer by layer, against the illusions that had wrapped themselves around my identity. Eternal Rest is not the absence of hardship—it's the intense release of everything that was never truly mine. To find it, I had to embark on the most challenging journey of all: deconditioning myself from the lies, expectations, and generational chains that sought to define me.

The process began with recognizing the noise that had shaped me—the societal scripts, the cultural expectations, the invisible rules whispered into my existence long before I had the chance to decide who I was. These whispers weren't mine, yet they guided my every move, keeping me bound to systems that thrived on conformity and self-sacrifice. "We can't find peace until we've sifted through the noise that tells us who we are." I realized that to rest, truly rest, I had to silence this noise and face the illusions head-on.

Generational cycles carry immense weight, and their unspoken traumas are passed down like heirlooms. They rope us to patterns we don't recognize until we've lived them. People-pleasing, codependency, the need to sacrifice for acceptance—these weren't just my struggles. They were echoes of my ancestors' survival mechanisms, passed through time as a form of protection but now outgrown. To break free, I had to name these chains for what they were: inherited pain, unprocessed grief, and cycles of fear.

"To heal, you must first confront the root, even when the root is tangled in generations of silence."

Breaking these cycles wasn't just about me. It was about the daughters I'm raising and the legacy I'm leaving. Each time I chose to let go of a pattern, I felt the weight of generations lifting, a ripple effect of freedom echoing into the future. I wasn't just healing myself; I was transforming the very foundation of what my lineage could be.

But healing wasn't a gentle process. It was rebellion—against systems, against expectations, and most profoundly, against my own conditioning. The world had taught me that rest was indulgent and that I had to earn my worth through service, sacrifice, and relentless effort. Choosing myself felt like a radical act, a refusal to abide by the rules that sought to diminish me.

"Choosing yourself is revolutionary when you've been conditioned to seek approval."

This rebellion demanded that I stop explaining myself. I had to unlearn the compulsion to justify every decision, to seek validation for every boundary I set. Not everyone will understand your healing, and not everyone is meant to. I came to realize that my rest, my peace, and my choices were not up for public debate. They were mine—sacred, untouchable, and wholly mine to hold.

True rest isn't the absence of movement or the stillness of sleep. It's the freedom from everything that weighs you down. It's choosing to release the expectations that suffocate, the relationships that drain, and the habits that hinder growth. Rest is the reward for releasing what no longer serves you.

In finding Eternal Rest, I learned to honor the quiet sanctuary within myself. This was not the peace that comes from the world but the peace that comes from reclaiming your spirit. It's the kind of rest that allows you to breathe deeply, to exist without apology, and to know that your worth is not tied to how much you produce or perform.

I now carry this rest with me, a lightness that reflects the work I've done. It shows up in how I move through the world—in the boundaries I protect, in the love I give myself, and in the freedom I refuse to compromise. This rest is not about stopping; it's about starting fresh, untethered from the past.

Eternal Rest is the reward for choosing yourself over and over again. It's the gift of peace earned through courage, self-reflection, and unwavering commitment to your own healing. It's the space where I stand now, whole and free, knowing that this rest isn't the end of the journey—it's the beginning of a life fully lived, unapologetically at peace.

CHAPTER 18
Soul Contract

The concept of soul contracts is more than an abstract idea—it's a framework for understanding the deeply transformative relationships and situations we encounter in life. These contracts aren't accidents; they are cosmic agreements designed to awaken us, heal us, and ultimately push us toward our highest potential. Each soul contract carries with it a lesson, a revelation, and a mirror that reflects the parts of ourselves we need to face—whether we're ready or not.

One of my most transformative awakenings came when I encountered the work of Caroline Myss, whose teachings on soul contracts redefined how I understood my relationships. Myss, a renowned medical intuitive and author, introduced the idea that these contracts are sacred assignments designed to challenge us, often through pain, and guide us toward self-discovery. Her insights gave me the language to decode my relationships, not as random connections but as pivotal turning points in my soul's journey.

"A soul contract," as Myss explains, "isn't an accident; it's a divine appointment with evolution, often delivered through pain, revelation, and self-confrontation."

Understanding the Contracts

Some soul contracts arrive as lovers, their presence igniting passion and vulnerability but also exposing our fears and insecurities. Others emerge as friendships, challenging us to grow beyond our comfort zones and forcing us to confront our blind spots. And sometimes, these contracts manifest through family, where love and judgment intertwine, offering profound lessons in boundaries and self-acceptance.

Each of these connections carries an energy that resonates deeply with our soul, acting as catalysts for growth. They force us to confront the parts of ourselves we'd rather ignore—the wounds, the patterns, and the insecurities that shape how we see the world.

The Defining Soul Contracts of My Life

1. The Partner Who Reflected My Attachments and Insecurities

One of my most powerful soul contracts came through a relationship that was as intoxicating as it was destructive. At the time, I mistook its intensity for love, but in truth, it was a mirror reflecting my unresolved attachments and deep-seated insecurities. This partner embodied everything I thought I needed, yet their presence revealed how much I had neglected my own needs in pursuit of external validation.

"Sometimes, the person we think we need is the one who shows us how little we are loving ourselves."

Through this relationship, I came face-to-face with my tendency to idealize, to cling to illusions, and to lose myself in the process. The pain of that connection forced me to reclaim my sense of self, teaching me that love begins within, not through someone else's approval.

2. The Friend Who Pushed Me to Grow Beyond Comfort

Another soul contract that left an indelible mark was with a friend who entered my life when I was stagnant and afraid to take risks. This friend's blunt honesty was both jarring and transformative. They challenged my beliefs, called out my excuses, and pushed me to step into my power.

"True friends are those who force us to face ourselves, even when it hurts."

Through them, I learned resilience, self-reliance, and the courage to confront my limitations. This friendship taught me that growth often comes from discomfort and that the people who truly care about us are the ones who encourage us to evolve, even when it's painful.

3. The Family Member Who Was My Mirror

The most challenging contracts often come through family, where expectations and love collide. For me, a close relative embodied traits I struggled to accept within myself, becoming a mirror for my own flaws and fears.

This relationship forced me to practice patience and compassion on a deeper level. It also taught me the necessity of boundaries—recognizing that even family members don't have the right to overstep the lines I've drawn to protect my peace.

"Boundaries are the unspoken love we give to both ourselves and others."

4. The Adversary Who Taught Me Forgiveness

One of the most unexpected soul contracts came in the form of an adversary—a person whose actions caused me pain but ultimately led to my greatest transformation. Through time and reflection, I found forgiveness for this person, not as an act of absolution for them but as a liberation for myself.

"Forgiveness is less about absolving others and more about freeing yourself."

This contract taught me that holding onto resentment only anchors us to the pain, while forgiveness creates space for healing and growth. It was a lesson in reclaiming my power, transforming anger into wisdom, and letting go of the weight I had carried for far too long.

The Lessons of Soul Contracts

I've learned through each of these contracts that relationships are sacred assignments, not destinations. They are designed to push us closer to our true selves, to challenge the narratives we've built, and to dismantle the illusions that keep us trapped.

Soul contracts are not always gentle. They demand that we look inward, face our shadows, and take responsibility for our healing. But they also offer immense gifts—resilience, forgiveness, self-awareness, and an unshakable sense of self-worth.

Choosing to Evolve

The beauty of soul contracts is that while they may begin with pain, they often end with clarity. They've shown me that every relationship is a reflection, a mirror that offers the chance to heal, to grow, and to love myself more deeply. Understanding these divine assignments has allowed me to embrace the complexities of my journey. Each soul I've encountered has been a teacher, and through their lessons, I've discovered the strength, love, and wisdom within me.

These contracts are not chains but keys—tools that unlock the doors to our highest potential. As I continue this journey, I carry with me the understanding that every soul I meet and every experience I endure is part of a greater design, guiding me home to myself.

CHAPTER 19
Hidden Beneath the Surface

Navigating the unseen has always been my reality—a delicate, intuitive dance where premonitions guide me through life's winding paths. My psychic abilities aren't just fleeting glimpses; they are the heartbeat of my existence, offering insights and answers that others might overlook. Each vision, each feeling, is like a whisper from beyond, guiding me, protecting me, and revealing what lies hidden beneath the surface.

For years, I thought these experiences made me different in a way that couldn't be explained. At times, I wondered if I was losing my mind. That all changed at 35 when I learned my grandfather was a psychic. Suddenly, the mysteries of my abilities didn't feel so isolating. For the first time, I had a connection to something larger than myself, something ancestral and rooted in my lineage. The answers I had been searching for were no longer shrouded in confusion. I wasn't "crazy"—I was carrying a gift that had been passed down through generations.

The Deepest Premonition

One of the most defining moments of my journey came with a premonition of an elementary school shooting. It struck me out of nowhere—a flash of terror and pain that I couldn't shake. I remember the exact moment it hit me, a wave of unease washing over me like a tidal force. At first, I dismissed it, telling myself I was overthinking and that I needed to calm down. But the feeling persisted, growing stronger until it became impossible to ignore.

Hours later, the news broke: the shooting had happened exactly as I had seen it. Social media and news outlets were flooded with the tragedy. That moment left me shaken to my core. The clarity of the vision was undeniable, but its weight was suffocating. I thought, *Am I supposed to carry this? What do I do with this ability?* I felt alone, disconnected, and unsure if I could handle the weight of my mind anymore. I contemplated checking myself into a psych hospital, convinced there was something wrong with me. My mind felt like an enemy I couldn't escape.

In those dark moments, my mom sat me down. Her words, simple yet profound, became a lifeline: "There is nothing wrong with you." That was the day she put her fears away from the psychic world she grew up in and told me that this gift wasn't a curse, even if it felt like one. Slowly, I began to see the truth in her words. The more spiritual I became—praying, affirming, fasting—the stronger my abilities grew. My connection deepened, and while that brought clarity, it also came with responsibility. I had to learn how to manage this gift, to discern when to lean into it, and when to create boundaries for my own peace.

The Pull

My abilities don't fit into a single box. They're layered and multifaceted, manifesting in ways I'm still discovering. Premonitions are one of the strongest threads—vivid, undeniable flashes of what's to come. Then there's the ability to feel energy in a room, to know what someone is holding onto without them ever saying a word. I've also experienced clairaudience, hearing the whispers of guidance that seem to come from nowhere yet carry profound truth. These abilities have shaped my life in ways I could never have imagined, forcing me to trust what I feel even when logic tries to tell me otherwise.

At times, my abilities have felt like a double-edged sword. I started noticing things I didn't want to see. I would pull visions from people—past events, secrets, pain—and it felt like my mind was working against me. Imagine knowing every time your partner was cheating. It wasn't just intuition; it was a relentless pull, an unfiltered stream of information that I couldn't turn off. I had to train my mind to stay grounded, to "mind my business" in a world where my gift constantly sought to reveal what lay hidden. Training my mind from my abilities never worked.

The Night in Lagos

One night in Lagos brought these gifts into sharp focus. My friends and I were heading out to a club, eager to escape into the energy of the night. As I sat in the passenger seat, something felt wrong—an invisible weight pressed against me, urging me to be cautious. I had an overwhelming urge not to drink that night. At first, I dismissed it, questioning why I felt so uneasy. But despite my doubts, I committed to staying sober. Little did I know that decision would save us.

As we drove through the dark, unmarked streets, the sense of danger grew stronger. Suddenly, a vision hit me like a bolt of lightning—a car accident, vivid and jarring. I could see it as if it were already happening: the screeching brakes, the crunch of metal, the chaos of impact. My focus locked onto a cement truck barreling down a bridge ahead, its speed far too fast for the turn it was taking. I shouted at the driver to slow down, snapping her attention away from her phone just in time. She swerved, narrowly avoiding a full collision, but the car flipped, rolling multiple times before coming to a stop. The wreckage was devastating, yet all of us emerged with only scratches. My intuition had saved us, and I could no longer deny its power.

The Girl in My Chair – Atlanta, 2012

In 2012, a young woman sat in my chair at my salon in Atlanta, carrying an unspoken question. She was nervous, unsure of herself, and hesitant to share what was on her mind. As I began working on her hair, I felt her curiosity and self-doubt. She was considering beauty school but doubted whether she had what it took to succeed. As she spoke, a vision began to form in my mind—clear and undeniable. I saw her future: a vibrant salon in Ghana, where she stood confidently, thriving in her craft.

I shared the vision with her, encouraging her to attend Aveda for training, knowing it would set her on the path I had seen. Four years later, she called me, her voice filled with gratitude and disbelief. She had graduated, opened her salon in Ghana, and was living the life we had talked about that day. Her success was a testament to the power of vision—not just mine but her own belief in what was possible.

Finding Balance

Knowing my grandfather shared this gift has anchored me. It's a reminder that I'm not alone in this journey and that my abilities are part of something much larger than myself. They're a legacy, a connection to the unseen, and a tool for transformation—not just for me but for those whose paths I cross.

These encounters have taught me that my gift isn't just about what I see—it's about how I use it. Whether it's saving lives, guiding others toward their purpose, or even navigating my own challenges, this gift is a compass. But I've learned that even a compass requires discipline. It's not about seeing everything but about knowing when to act, when to step back, and when to let the vision unfold naturally.

I've also learned the importance of creating boundaries—not just with others but within myself. I no longer allow my gift to overwhelm me. I've embraced practices that ground me, rituals that allow me to recharge and remain in control. This isn't just about managing my gift; it's about honoring it. It's about recognizing that while I have the ability to see beyond the surface, I also have the responsibility to protect my peace.

The journey of navigating the unseen isn't easy, but it's one I wouldn't trade. It has shown me that even in moments of doubt, confusion, and fear, there is purpose. It has taught me that we all carry gifts—whether seen or unseen—and that those gifts are meant to serve not just ourselves but the greater good.

Now, when I feel the pull of a vision, I don't fight it or fear it. I honor it, trusting that it's guiding me toward something meaningful. My mind, once an enigma I struggled to understand, has become my ally. It's a part of me—a powerful, transformative part—that I've learned to embrace fully.

What lies hidden beneath the surface isn't meant to be feared. It's meant to be uncovered, explored, and cherished. And in doing so, I've found not just answers but a profound sense of self—a clarity that no vision could ever replace.

CHAPTER 20
Reclaiming My Sovereignty

A new understanding began to emerge from the quiet healing of my solitude. I had spent chapters of my life peeling back layers, facing shadows, and relearning how to love myself. Each step brought me closer to reclaiming something I had unknowingly surrendered—a sacred right to fully own my choices, my energy, and my boundaries. Sovereignty was not just a concept; it was the culmination of everything I had been working toward, the embodiment of standing unshaken in my truth.

Friendships had always been a part of my story. In earlier chapters, they mirrored my insecurities, amplified my wounds, and often blurred the lines of who I was. But now, they have become a testament to my transformation. My Libra placement in the 11th house, with Scorpio's and Pluto's influence creating an "open door," once allowed others' energies to pour into me unchecked. I had unknowingly invited people into my life who reflected unresolved parts of myself—people who demanded more than they offered and connections that drained rather than nourished.

One friendship stood out. For years, I tolerated emotional manipulation disguised as loyalty. It was met with guilt-tripping or passive-aggressive remarks whenever I set a boundary. Yet, I stayed, believing that my willingness to endure made me a good friend. It wasn't until I sat in the stillness of my solitude that I realized I had been giving away my power in exchange for validation. I was showing up for others in ways they never showed up for me.

Reclaiming my sovereignty meant redefining these relationships—not with resentment, but with clarity. I learned that boundaries are not walls but filters, allowing only what aligns with my highest good to pass through. Also, understanding evolution has stages and also requires letting go for greater to come in. One by one, I began letting go of connections that no longer served me. Some exits were quiet, others abrupt, but each departure made space for something more aligned.

True sovereignty isn't about isolating yourself; it's about standing firmly in your truth and knowing your worth no matter what. Solitude became my training ground. In the silence, I could hear my voice clearly for the first time, free from the noise of others' expectations. I no longer needed external validation because I had found an unshakable confidence in who I was.

The Power of Choosing Myself

In one pivotal moment, I encountered someone who challenged this newfound strength. They were magnetic, persuasive, and had an uncanny ability to make me question my boundaries. But this time was different. As they tried to edge past the limits I had set, I felt a calm resolve wash over me. I didn't need to argue or justify myself—I simply held my ground.

For the first time, I saw boundaries not as acts of defiance but as acts of self-love. Saying "no" without guilt, removing myself from toxic dynamics, and prioritizing my peace felt like revolutionary acts in a world that had taught me to give endlessly. At that moment, I understood sovereignty as an internal compass, guiding me to protect what I had worked so hard to reclaim.

From Trauma Bonds to True Connections

The more I embraced my sovereignty, the more I saw how it transformed the energy around me. Relationships that thrived on control or dependency began to dissolve, replaced by connections rooted in mutual respect and authenticity. For the first time, I was surrounded by people who saw my worth without me having to prove it, who celebrated my boundaries rather than testing them.

Sovereignty also reshaped how I viewed love and friendship. I no longer sought approval or permission to exist as I was. Instead, I attracted relationships that honored my wholeness, connections that didn't require me to shrink or sacrifice. This was freedom—standing tall in my truth while inviting only those who aligned with my energy to join me.

Closing the Open Door

The "open door" that once allowed others to walk in and out of my life unchecked is now closed—but not locked. It opens selectively, with intention and discernment. Reclaiming my sovereignty didn't mean shutting the world out; it meant curating the energy I allowed into my sacred space.

This journey has taught me that sovereignty is not about control but about choice. It's the choice to protect my peace, honor my growth, and live unapologetically in alignment with my truth. It's the realization that I am not here to be everything for everyone. I am here to be whole, to shine, and to create a life that reflects the fullness of who I am.

Sovereignty is my declaration that I am enough. I don't need external validation, and I don't need to explain myself. My worth is inherent, my energy sacred, and my path uniquely mine. This is what it means to reclaim my sovereignty—to live fully, fiercely, and freely as the woman I was always meant to be.

CHAPTER 21
Rival: Turning Pain to Power

The silence of healing is deceptive; it whispers truths that, at first, you might not want to hear. It pulls you into corners of your being where the rawness of your experiences waits, unhealed and unresolved. This chapter began in that silence, transitioning me from the reclamation of my sovereignty into a confrontation with an age-old rival: pain.

Pain isn't just a fleeting emotion; it is an experience that demands to be felt. For years, I ran from it, suppressed it, and allowed it to define me without understanding its purpose. Pain became my rival not because it sought to destroy me but because it refused to let me remain the same. It demanded growth, evolution, and transformation.

Pain came to me in the form of heartbreak—love that felt like fire but left ashes in its wake. It came through betrayal, the sting of trusting too much, only to be left questioning everything. Pain introduced itself in friendships where loyalty felt one-sided and in family dynamics that often blurred the lines of love and expectation. I spent years carrying these wounds, mistaking them for a part of my identity until I realized they were not scars to hold but lessons to release.

The most profound realization came when I stopped seeing pain as something inflicted on me and started seeing it as a force working through me. Pain wasn't here to punish me; it was here to teach me. The heartbreaks weren't just endings—they were beginnings. The betrayals weren't just losses—they were clarifications. Every moment of suffering was a call to rise above, to stop allowing external circumstances to dictate my internal world.

The Process of Transformation

Turning pain into power wasn't an easy feat. It required facing my rival head-on, peeling back every layer of avoidance and denial. I began to sit with my pain, truly sit with it. In the stillness, I allowed myself to cry, to feel, to mourn what was lost, and to acknowledge the parts of myself I had abandoned in the process.

Sitting alone in my room, there was a moment when I looked at myself in the mirror and saw not weakness but resilience. My tears weren't signs of defeat—they were symbols of strength, of a soul that refused to stay broken. I decided then that I wouldn't just survive my pain; I would alchemize it.

I started writing letters to the pain, addressing it as if it were a person. I thanked it for the lessons, acknowledged its presence, and then declared my freedom from it. Each letter felt like a weight lifting, a piece of myself returning. Slowly, I began to see the beauty in the process. Pain, when faced with courage, becomes a sculptor, shaping you into someone you didn't know you could be.

The Rival Within

The hardest part of this journey wasn't forgiving others; it was forgiving myself. I had to forgive the version of me who allowed mistreatment, who stayed too long in toxic spaces, who confused love with attachment. My fiercest rival wasn't the pain itself but the part of me that clung to it, that allowed it to define my worth.

It wasn't easy to let go of the stories I had told myself about who I was and what I deserved. But as I released the narratives that no longer served me, I felt a new kind of strength emerge—a strength rooted not in avoidance but in acceptance.

I began setting boundaries, not just with others but with myself. I stopped allowing self-doubt to creep in and poison my progress. I stopped revisiting old wounds just to feel their sting. I chose to move forward, carrying the lessons but leaving the pain behind.

Harnessing the Power

Today, I see pain as a force, not a foe. It's not something to fear but something to harness. The same energy that once broke me now fuels me, driving me to create, to love, and to live with intention. Pain taught me resilience, empathy, and the importance of self-mastery. It showed me that true power isn't about avoiding hardship—it's about rising from it, stronger and more aligned than ever before.

This journey from pain to power isn't linear, and it's not without setbacks. There are days when the shadows return, whispering doubts and fears. But even in those moments, I remind myself that I've faced my rival and emerged victorious. I've learned to take every setback and use it as fuel for my growth, turning what once hurt me into the foundation of my strength.

The Glow of Transformation

Now, when I walk into a room, I carry not just my light but the depth of my journey. My glow isn't just brightness—it's layers of resilience, courage, and self-discovery. Pain didn't break me; it revealed me. It stripped away everything I wasn't and left behind the woman I was always meant to be.

This chapter isn't just about turning pain into power—it's about honoring the process, embracing the rival within, and using every scar as a testament to the strength that lies hidden beneath the surface. Pain, once a rival, is now my ally, a force that keeps me grounded, humbled, and fiercely alive.

CHAPTER 22
The Day I Met My Soul

Some moments arrive like whispers, barely noticeable yet utterly transformative. This was one of those moments—a quiet reckoning that pulled me inward, past the noise of life and into the stillness of my own being. It didn't come with fireworks or grand gestures. It came softly, patiently, as if it had been waiting for me to listen finally.

The day I met my soul was not marked on any calendar. It wasn't a milestone or a dramatic turning point. Instead, it unfolded in the midst of surrender. I had spent so much of my life running—running from pain, from expectations, from myself. But in the stillness of that day, something shifted. I stopped running. I let the silence envelop me, and for the first time, I allowed myself to simply be.

The Encounter

It was subtle at first, like a warmth spreading from within, a presence that felt deeply familiar yet wholly profound. I wasn't meeting someone new; I was rediscovering someone I had always been. It felt as though my soul had been waiting for this very moment, whispering gently, *"I've been here all along."*

As the layers of distraction fell away, I began to see myself clearly—not as a collection of roles, achievements, or failures, but as something deeper. Beneath the pain, the triumphs, the masks I had worn for survival, there was a light, unbroken and unshaken. Meeting my soul was like coming home after years of wandering, finally stepping into the essence of who I truly am.

In that moment, I felt an overwhelming sense of peace. My soul didn't demand answers or explanations. It didn't judge me for the choices I had made or the paths I had taken. It simply existed, unwavering and complete, showing me that I, too, am complete.

The Lessons

My soul didn't speak in words but in knowing. It revealed that the pain I had endured wasn't a punishment but a teacher. Every heartbreak, every loss, every moment of uncertainty—they weren't detours; they were initiations. They had stripped me of what was false and brought me closer to my truth.

Meeting my soul taught me that the love I had sought from others—the validation, the acceptance—had always been within me. It wasn't something to be earned or given; it was something to be claimed. I realized that my soul had never been broken, only buried beneath layers of conditioning, fear, and doubt.

This encounter was a reckoning with vulnerability. For years, I had worn armor to protect myself from the world, but in doing so, I had also shielded myself from my own essence. My soul showed me that true strength lies not in the armor but in the courage to lay it down, to stand raw and open, unafraid of my depth.

The Partnership

The day I met my soul wasn't just a moment—it was the beginning of a lifelong partnership. My soul became my compass, my guide, and my anchor. It reminded me that no matter how chaotic the world may become, I have a sanctuary within me, a place of unwavering truth and strength.

I now understand that my soul isn't separate from me; it is me. It is the part of me that knows, that loves, that exists beyond the fleeting challenges of this life. It is the source of my creativity, resilience, and purpose.

Moving Forward

Since that day, I have lived differently. I no longer search outward for validation or answers. Everything I need is within me, waiting to be acknowledged. My decisions are no longer driven by fear or insecurity but by quiet confidence from knowing who I am.

The day I met my soul wasn't the end of my journey but the beginning. It was the moment I stopped surviving and started living—from a place of authenticity, the unshakable foundation of my being.

This chapter of my life is a testament to the power of self-discovery. It's a reminder that beneath the noise, the distractions, and the pain, there is a light within each of us waiting to be seen. The day I met my soul was when I stepped into my power, truth, and infinite potential.

"To meet your soul is to find the part of you that is eternal, unbroken, and whole. It is when you stop searching and finally see yourself as you truly are."

CHAPTER 23

The Rise & Rebirth of the Sleeping Phoenix

There is a power within us—a force that lies dormant, waiting for the right moment to awaken and claim its place in the world. That force was my Sleeping Phoenix, the essence of my resilience, creativity, and strength. It had always been there, quietly gathering energy, waiting for the flames to ignite its rebirth.

This chapter is not just about survival; it's about transformation. It's about burning away the illusions, the expectations, and the limitations that no longer served me and rising into the woman I was always meant to be. To understand the rise of my Phoenix, you must understand the ashes it emerged from—the trials, the heartaches, and the moments of profound surrender that made this rebirth possible.

Confronting the Flames

The flames came in waves: heartbreaks that shattered me, friendships that dissolved under the weight of truth, and moments when I felt utterly lost. These weren't just challenges; they were initiations, demanding that I confront my fears and strip away the false identities I had clung to for so long.

There was a time when I feared the fire. I saw it as destruction, a force that could consume me. But as I walked through it, I began to see it differently. The flames weren't there to destroy me; they were there to cleanse me, to burn away everything that wasn't true to who I am. It was painful, yes, but it was also liberating.

I had to let go of the parts of me that sought approval and prioritized others' comfort over my truth. I had to release the fear of being too much—too intense, too passionate, too different. The fire demanded my surrender, and I found my power in surrendering.

The Stirring of the Phoenix

As the flames subsided, I felt a stirring within me—a quiet but undeniable energy, a force that had been dormant for so long. This was my Sleeping Phoenix, reawakening with a power I hadn't known before. It wasn't just fierce but also tender, a balance of strength and vulnerability that felt deeply authentic.

This energy was a reclamation of my true self. The emotions I once saw as weaknesses—my sensitivity, depth, and yearning for something greater—were revealed as my greatest strengths. They were the fuel for my fire, the essence of what made me unstoppable.

The Phoenix within me rose, carrying with it the wisdom of every lesson I had learned: that pain is a teacher, that vulnerability is strength, and that the only way to rise is to embrace every part of who you are—light and shadow, strength and softness.

The Power of Rebirth

The rebirth of the Sleeping Phoenix was not a single moment; it was a process, a series of choices to trust myself, to let go of what no longer served me, and to step boldly into my power. I stopped apologizing for my vision, my intensity, and my fire. Instead, I embraced them as gifts, as the very qualities that make me who I am.

Each scar became a badge of honor, each fall a stepping stone, and each lesson a reminder of my resilience. The rebirth was not about becoming someone new but about returning to who I have always been, the woman I was before the world told me who I should be.

A New Beginning

The Sleeping Phoenix is no longer dormant. It is alive, vibrant, and unyielding, a symbol of the endless cycle of transformation that defines my journey. I am no longer bound by the past but empowered by it. The ashes of yesterday have become the foundation for the woman I am today—a force of nature, a soul unafraid to rise again and again, each time stronger, each time more authentic.

As I soar into this new chapter, I carry the lessons, the wisdom, and the fire that will guide me forward. The rise and rebirth of the Sleeping Phoenix is not just a personal triumph but a testament to the power of transformation, a celebration of the strength within us all.

"To rise as a Phoenix is to embrace the flames, to let them refine you, and to soar with the unshakable knowing that you are, and have always been, enough."

CHAPTER 24
Letter to Self

Dear Me,

Let's stop pretending. Stop apologizing. Stop hiding. You've spent too many years trying to fit into a world never built to hold you. You've carried their expectations like chains, judgments like weights, and opinions like gospel. But here's the truth: *you were never meant to be tamed.*

Those pieces of you that felt "too much"? They were never flaws; they were flames. The world tried to snuff them out because they didn't know how to handle your heat. But you? You kept burning. Quietly. Relentlessly. Waiting for the moment you'd finally step into the firestorm of your truth.

And here you are.

Do you realize how extraordinary you are? How every scar you once tried to hide is a mark of survival, a testament to the wars you fought—and won? They called you difficult because you wouldn't bend. They called you rebellious because you refused to conform. But you're not difficult; you're decisive. You're not rebellious; you're revolutionary. And those who can't see it? They don't deserve a seat at your table.

You've lived through storms that would have broken lesser souls. You've carried the weight of heartbreak, betrayal, and rejection—and still, you rose. You didn't just survive; you thrived. You turned every tear into a river of strength, every doubt into a weapon, and every setback into a stepping stone. You are a masterpiece painted in resilience and raw power.

I'm sorry.

I'm sorry for the times I doubted you, for the moments I chose silence when you needed to roar. I'm sorry for believing the lies—that you were too much, not enough, or somehow wrong just for existing in your fullness. I'm sorry for letting fear hold you back when you were born to fly.

But here's the thing: you don't need my apology. You've already forgiven me. Because even when I failed to see you, *you always saw yourself.* You knew, deep down, that you were destined for more. That your story wasn't one of survival—it was one of domination.

You are the storm.

They won't see you coming. They'll underestimate you, try to define you, but you'll move through them like wildfire—uncontainable, undeniable, unstoppable. You are not for the faint of heart. You are for those who dare to stand in the glow of your power without flinching.

Your story doesn't end here; it begins. Because now, you own it—all of it. The pain, the triumphs, the moments that broke you, and the ones that rebuilt you. You've forged every piece of your journey into something unshakable.

And as you rise, you are the phoenix—shining bright, radiant with purpose, emerging from the ashes of a world that tried to bury you. You wings, forged in fire, stretch wide, unbound, and unstoppable, cast ing light over everything the darkness attempted to consume. You are proof that destruction is not the end but the beginning.

So walk into every room like you own it—because you do. Speak your truth, even when it makes the earth tremble. You are not here to fit in; you are here to set the standard, to rewrite the rules, to break the damn mold.

And when they ask, "Who does she think she is?" you'll look them dead in the eye and say, *"I am the phoenix, and I rise."*

With every ounce of fire,

Your Soul

About the Author

Osasere Cynthia Omorodion is a spiritual personologist, transformation coach, writer, and serial entrepreneur, deeply committed to guiding others toward self-discovery and authentic living. A continuous-
generation energy reader, Osasere comes from a long line of psychics,
each generation in her lineage passing down powerful, intuitive gifts.
This legacy has become the foundation of her work, inspiring her to
help others uncover and harness their inner truth.

With a multifaceted approach to personal insight, Osasere blends
Human Design, astrology, numerology, and palmistry as a personality
analyst to reveal each client's unique path and purpose. Through her
transformative coaching, she provides motivation and guidance for
those ready to shed old layers, confront hidden truths, and step boldly
into their highest selves.

As a serial entrepreneur, she founded *Nature's Healing Exchange,*
wellness brand dedicated to natural healing, bridging her commitment
to holistic health and spiritual wellness. Osasere's ventures embody her

vision of supporting others in body, mind, and spirit, offering practical tools for personal growth.

In *Hidden in Plain Sight,* she bares her soul, sharing a raw journey of trials, triumphs, and awakening moments. Her fearless storytelling calls readers to honor their own journeys, embrace their rare spirit, and rise with newfound strength. Osasere's words are both a personal revelation and a powerful invitation to discover your truest self, and her work continues to inspire those ready to evolve and live fully.

Read more at itscoachosas.com.

www.ingramcontent.com/pod-product-compliance
Lightning Source LLC
Chambersburg PA
CBHW061337140726

47997CB00003B/1008